THE EVERYTHING®

GUIDE TO SMOKING FOOD

Dear Reader,

If you're new to smoking foods, this book is for you. I didn't write this book for the experienced backyard pit master or the competition barbecue pit master. I wrote it for the novice smoker looking for techniques, tips, and ideas for cooking delicious smoked foods.

It's my hope this book will inspire you to create great tasting dishes for your friends, family, and guests. Once you've got the basics down from this book, start building on your knowledge and skills by experimenting with new recipes and techniques. Eventually you'll get to the point where smoking food is more than just a hobby, it's a lifestyle. Enjoy the journey!

Larry

Welcome to the EVERYTHING® Series!

These handy, accessible books give you all you need to tackle a difficult project, gain a new hobby, comprehend a fascinating topic, prepare for an exam, or even brush up on something you learned back in school but have since forgotten.

You can choose to read an Everything® book from cover to cover or just pick out the information you want from our three useful boxes: e-questions, e-facts, and e-ssentials. We give you everything you need to know on the subject, but throw in a lot of fun stuff along the way, too.

We now have more than 400 Everything® books in print, spanning such wide-ranging categories as weddings, pregnancy, cooking, music instruction, foreign language, crafts, pets, New Age, and so much more. When you're done reading them all, you can finally say you know Everything®!

QUESTION

Answers to common questions

FACT

Important snippets of information

ESSENTIAL

Quick handy tips

PUBLISHER Karen Cooper

MANAGING EDITOR, EVERYTHING® SERIES Lisa Laing

COPY CHIEF Casey Ebert

ASSISTANT PRODUCTION EDITOR Alex Guarco

ACQUISITIONS EDITOR Lisa Laing

ASSOCIATE DEVELOPMENT EDITOR Eileen Mullan

EVERYTHING® SERIES COVER DESIGNER Erin Alexander

Visit the entire Everything® series at *www.everything.com*

THE
EVERYTHING®
GUIDE TO
SMOKING FOOD

All you need to cook with smoke—indoors or out!

Larry Gaian

Avon, Massachusetts

This book is dedicated to my wife, Celeste. Her love, support,
and inspiration have made everything I do possible.

Published by
Adams Media, a division of F+W Media, Inc.
57 Littlefield Street, Avon, MA 02322. U.S.A.
www.adamsmedia.com

ISBN 10: 1-4405-7298-4
ISBN 13: 978-1-4405-7298-2
eISBN 10: 1-4405-7299-2
eISBN 13: 978-1-4405-7299-9

Printed in the United States of America.

10 9 8 7 6 5 4 3 2 1

Always follow safety and commonsense cooking protocol while using kitchen utensils, operating ovens and stoves, and handling uncooked food. If children are assisting in the preparation of any recipe, they should always be supervised by an adult.

Photographs by Kelly Jaggers.
Cover images © Elena Shashkina/123RF; © StockFood/Erricson, Colin/
Poplis, Paul/Ernalbant, Emel.

This book is available at quantity discounts for bulk purchases.
For information, please call 1-800-289-0963.

Contents

Acknowledgments

Adam Perry Lang, probably without knowing it, has been my inspiration. His cookbooks, recipes, and conversations have given me the desire and skills to try new and exciting foods outdoors.

A lot of what I know I learned from my friends at The BBQ Brethren. Their friendship and skills have always been shared without hesitation. Thanks, Phil.

And especially Mary, my mother, who has shown me what it is to be strong and to persevere.

Introduction

While this book does contain grilling techniques and tips, this isn't a book solely about barbecuing and grilling. It's about one of the oldest cooking processes on earth—smoking.

For years now, people all over the world have been using the flavors of smoke to enhance meals. Today smoke is still used as a preservative to a small extent, but for the most part, it's used to make foods taste better. In fact, smoke can be considered an ingredient in its own right. Herbs, spices, and other ingredients in a recipe meld together in a kind of chemical reaction to make food taste delicious. Smoke is just one more element that adds a layer of flavor.

Don't be intimated, though. Adding smoke flavor to foods doesn't mean you have to spend eighteen hours watching over a barbecue pit tending the heat, wood, and meat. Adding smoke to something delicate like a scallop so it has a hint of apple wood sweetness is just as rewarding—and far less time-consuming.

In this book, you're going to learn how much fun adding smoke to your foods can be. Smoking foods doesn't require fancy equipment. You can smoke something with a couple of charcoal briquettes and some wood chips wrapped in foil. There is a good chance most of the tools you need to start smoking a variety of foods are already in your pantry, garage, or patio. You can even use a stovetop smoker to create delicious smoked foods indoors!

Whether it's with a coffee can and a couple of hot briquettes and wood chips or a giant mobile barbecue pit that costs as much as a car, the techniques for creating smoke are not much different. Heat, wood, and just a little oxygen are all you need to make smoke.

The recipes found in this book demonstrate a variety of smoking techniques and equipment, from tea smoking using a wok to low-and-slow cooking in a backyard smoker. Remember, these techniques and flavors are easily mixed together. Use these recipes as a guide—mix and match different wood smoke flavors, spices, herbs, and other ingredients. Experiment with different combinations of meats, vegetables, marinades, rubs, and sauces. Try different techniques and woods to create your own signature smoke flavor. When it comes to smoking your own foods, there really should be only one rule, and that is: have fun with it!

CHAPTER 1

Introduction to Smoked Foods

Smoke adds a layer of flavor to foods that, for many people, is the essence of comfort. What was once an essential technique for preserving foods has evolved into a cooking process that is now, for the most part, done to please your taste buds. Smoking is one of the easiest ways to add flavor to foods and can make even the most inexperienced cook look and feel like an expert.

The History of Smoked Foods

The technique of smoking foods can be traced back to the time when people lived in caves. As hunters hung meat in the cave to dry, they learned that the meat hung closer to a fire would absorb the fire's smoke. The meat that dried closer to the fire would be better preserved than meat hung farther away—and it tasted different as well.

As mankind moved out of caves and into huts or tents, food preservation became more important. A nomadic lifestyle meant meat might not always be readily available, and keeping spoilage to a minimum was vital to survival. Smoking helped solve this problem. For example, the Native Americans of the Pacific Northwest have smoked their annual salmon catch for years by tying the fish to cedar boards and drying them over an open fire. Drying and smoking the salmon gave them the ability to store their fish for the long winters.

QUESTION

Is there really a difference between barbecue and grilling?
Technically there is a difference, from a traditional standpoint. Barbecue is cooking with indirect heat using a low-and-slow method, while grilling is high-heat cooking directly over the heat source. But if you're in your backyard grilling steaks and want to call it a barbecue, go right ahead!

Eventually, as curing meats in salt and brines became more popular, the combination of salt and smoke was used to increase the effectiveness of meat preservation. When the refrigerator was developed and then combined with modern transportation modes, salting, curing, and smoking became less of a need. Instead, smoking is now used to enhance the flavor of food. Additionally, smoking meats is a popular way to tenderize cheaper, tougher cuts of meat.

Evolution of Smoking Styles and Tools

The ancestry of the modern-day smoker can be traced back to the invention of the Torry Kiln, which was built at the Research Center Torry in

Aberdeen, Scotland, in 1939. The Torry Kiln made large-scale smoking possible. Prior to the development of the Torry Kiln, smoke moved through the smoker using natural draft, meaning the air moved from the bottom of the smoker to the top, with no way to control humidity. Instead, the Torry Kiln used a series of motor-driven fans, heaters, temperature sensors, and air diffusers to control the amount of smoke.

It is not known where the term *barbecue* first came from, but there are plenty of educated guesses. For example, the ship logs of Christopher Columbus contain several references to the natives on the island of Hispaniola cooking over open fires. They referred to this style of cooking as "barbecoa."

This style of cooking eventually made it to the southern region of America, where slaves used the techniques imported from the islands and combined them with the spices and flavors they brought with them from Africa. At around the same time, the open-pit method of cooking became popular along the Mexican border, using the spices and flavors of that country. Just as the United States is considered a "melting pot," barbecue is a "melting pot" of flavors, cooking styles, and spices from all around the world.

FACT

Another theory regarding where the word *barbecue* came from is that the term originated from the French phrase "barbe a queue," which means "from head to tail."

Smoking Is Hot Right Now

Thanks to television, smoking is now one of the hottest food trends in the United States and abroad. American-style barbecue has become a comfort-food staple in many European countries. You can even find American-style barbecue restaurants in Japan and China.

Some of the most popular TV cooking shows feature smoked foods. There are barbecue competition shows and reality shows, and shows featuring chefs who use modern-day smoking techniques to infuse mild smoke flavors into their foods—all of which can easily be recreated in the home.

BBQ Pitmasters on Destination America Network is one of the more popular barbecue shows. This competition show demonstrates the talents of some of the best restaurant and competition barbecue circuit pit masters in the United States and Canada.

In addition, the competition barbecue circuit has never been more popular. The Kansas City Barbecue Society has almost 2,500 team names registered and sanctions over 200 competitions a year. Almost every state or region in the United States has its own barbecue association. And some of the most passionate and talented smoked food enthusiasts live in European countries. Teams from Denmark, the Netherlands, and England have been successful in some of the most prestigious barbecue competitions all over the world.

The trend only seems to be growing. Websites and blogs dedicated to smoking foods are some of the most popular websites on the Internet. Barbecue forums, where members trade recipes and teach each other techniques and skills for smoking, are popular destinations for new and experienced chefs alike.

The Temperatures of Smoke

There are three temperature ranges for smoking foods. Keep in mind that the temperature mentioned isn't actually the temperature of the smoke, but more importantly, the temperature of the air that surrounds the food in the cooking chamber of the smoker, also known as ambient temperature. Smoke doesn't cook anything. The heat that accompanies the smoke does. Why is this important to understand? Because there are some foods that you don't want to cook while smoking. If you've decided you want to try your hand at making the perfect smoked Gouda or Cheddar for macaroni cheese, you don't want to cook your cheese while smoking, so it's important to know the ambient temperature.

What about the wonderful bacon you've taken the time to cure? Cooking it while smoking would just deny you the joy of frying up a pan of bacon on the stove and enjoying the aroma later. However, if you've got yourself a giant fifteen-pound brisket, you aren't going to want to cold smoke it, because it would never reach the temperature you need to break down the collagens. Instead, you'll want to put it on the smoker for eighteen hours at a higher temperature.

Cold Smoke

The technique of using cold smoke is employed primarily to add a light smoke flavor to foods without actually cooking it. Almost anything can be cold smoked to some degree: Pork, seafood, beef, poultry, vegetables, and cheeses are a just a few examples.

One of the best things about cold smoking is that it can be done at a relatively inexpensive price. You don't need expensive equipment: A cardboard box or newly purchased five-gallon paint bucket from the local hardware store are all you need—along with the knowledge of how to create heatless smoke, of course.

It is possible to keep the cost down because you aren't cooking the food with an open flame, just smoke.

ESSENTIAL

Only use cardboard boxes or plastic buckets for cold smoking. Since the temperature from the heat source doesn't go above 85°F and there isn't an open flame, you can safely use carboard and plastic.

The smoke used in cold smoking is either generated with equipment and techniques designed to provide an unheated smoke, or created through traditional methods and allowed to cool before it reaches the food. Cold smoking is normally done at ambient temperatures between 65°F and 85°F (20°C–30°C). At these temperatures, the food will take on the smoke flavor, but will not be cooked. It will stay moist and raw-looking. If the foods have not been cured prior to cold smoking, they will need to be cooked in some manner before eating.

Hot Smoke

Foods that have been hot smoked are usually fully cooked when the smoking process is completed. The foods may be reheated, grilled, or fried after smoking, but they are typically okay to eat without any additional cooking. Hot-smoked foods include popular things like hams and some sausages.

Smoking foods at temperatures in the 126°F–176°F (52°C–80°C) range allows the smoke to enhance the flavor of the food while keeping the food moist and without the shrinkage you would normally get from smoking foods at a higher temperature. At these mid-level temperatures, the flavorful fats will not render out of the meat. Fats in sausages, hams, and other similar products are vital to the flavor when cooking or reheating. Smoking the hams and other meats at these temperatures will allow the smoke to flavor the meat without rendering all the fat from the meat.

Smoke Roasting or Barbecue

Smoking at higher temperatures, typically above 200°F (93°C), is commonly known as barbecuing. When cooking at these temperatures you are roasting your food with heat, just as you would in your oven, except you have the benefit of the additional smoke flavor.

This method of cooking is normally done outdoors using a barbecue pit or smoker of some type. However, it can be accomplished indoors with proper ventilation and the correct tools. Smoking foods in a conventional oven should only be done in a well-ventilated area to avoid carbon monoxide poisoning.

In many parts of the world barbecuing and grilling are the same thing, but they are different processes. Grilling is normally a "hot-and-fast" method, while barbecuing is considered "low-and-slow." For example, if a whole chicken is grilled over direct heat, it will take somewhere in the neighborhood of 30 minutes. If the same chicken is barbecued "low-and-slow," the cooking time jumps to between 3 and 4 hours, depending upon the size of the chicken. You can add smoke flavor while grilling using wood chips, pellets, or wood planks.

Direct Heat versus Indirect Heat

Generating smoke outdoors can be accomplished using several different methods. Whether you choose to smoke your foods on a grill, smoker, or some other device, you will use either a direct or indirect heat source.

Knowing whether to use direct or indirect heat to smoke your food is an essential part of being a great cook.

Direct Heat

Direct-heat cooking is the easiest and simplest of all cooking methods. Foods are cooked directly over the heat source. The best example of direct-heat cooking is grilling. When you grill, foods are placed on grates directly above the hot charcoal or gas flames. This is the way most people cook hamburgers or a juicy rib eye steak. Because the food is quickly seared, direct-heat cooking is the least effective method for adding smoke flavor to your foods. In order for smoke to penetrate the meat, it needs a surface that will allow the penetration. When the meat is seared, the charring of the skin or meat surface forms a barrier to the smoke. You certainly can smoke the meat after searing, but your smoke flavor will be only on the surface of the meat.

Although it's not impossible to do, adding a smoke flavor to grilled foods using direct heat can be challenging. Combining the great flavor of direct-heat-cooked foods with the enhanced flavor of smoke can be accomplished by combining two cooking techniques. Try cold or hot smoking your foods before grilling. This will impart the smoke flavor while giving you the ability to get the great taste of grilled foods.

Indirect Heat

Indirect cooking uses radiant heat to cook the food. Radiant heat is the most common form of heating. Simply, it is the act of heating the air around you or something else. For example, the oven in your kitchen cooks using indirect radiant heat. The heat is circulated around the food, which in turn cooks the food from all sides at the same time. Indirect heat is great for smoking foods. Since the food is cooking more slowly with an indirect heat source, the food has time to pick up more smoke flavor.

Indirect-heat cooking is accomplished outdoors using an offset smoker or barbecue pit. With this equipment, the heat source is located in the fire box, which is normally shielded from where the food is placed. This allows greater control over the fire, while also allowing the food to cook with hot air.

You can accomplish the same thing using your charcoal or gas grill by piling your charcoal up on the sides of the grill, leaving the center empty.

With a gas grill, turning on one set of burners at the opposite end of the grill from where the food is cooking will also give you indirect heat.

The Four Regional Barbecue Styles and Flavors

Barbecue! For many people, this cooking method is synonymous with smoked foods. The combination of wood smoke, seasonings, and sauce perfectly illustrates why adding smoke to one food can enhance and complement the other foods on your plate.

Even though there are many different regional styles of barbecue depending on where you might be in the world, it is widely accepted that there are four main styles of American barbecue. Most other styles are a combination of these or are adapted to fit local food and flavor choices.

Texas

Texas-style barbecue is probably best known for its beef—especially beef brisket. Actually, Texas is big enough to have two very different barbecue styles.

Central Texas

During the 1800s, German, Czech, and other European immigrants settled in the central Texas area that now includes the cities of Lockhart, Luling, and Taylor. This is where the tradition of serving smoked meats out of meat markets on plain butcher paper was started. Although the tradition of serving the food on butcher paper continues, the railroad and other workers are no longer required to go to the back door of the restaurant to receive their lunches of beef brisket and beef sausage.

In Central Texas barbecue, the meats are seasoned simply, with lots of salt and pepper and maybe a few herbs or spices, and are smoked in old-fashioned brick-pit ovens. This style of barbecue is all about the meat, so much so that the meat is served on trays covered in butcher paper, sometimes with a few slices of white bread and maybe a fork. Pickles, jalapeños, onions, and carrots are usually served on the side as well.

The sauce, if it's served at all, is put on the side for dipping the meat into. Central Texas barbecue sauce is usually a thin, tomato-based sauce with just a slight amount of sweetness and spice. In this region, the sauce is not as important as the flavor of the meat.

East Texas

Unlike the barbecue in the Central Valley of Texas, which is mainly beef and sliced, East Texas barbecue is usually pork or beef that is chopped and served on a bun with a thick, sweet sauce. The East Texas style of barbecue is closest to other Southern styles of barbecue and is the most popular in the bigger cities of Texas.

The East Texas barbecue style is heavily influenced by African American culture. Beef and pork are usually chopped instead of sliced, and then served on a bun. Hot sauce also plays an important part in serving the chopped meat. There is a theory that hot sauce became popular because escaped or freed slaves had to eat cheaper, tougher cuts of meat, so they chopped up the meat to make it more edible and doused it in hot sauce to cover up the bad taste.

Memphis

Memphis-style barbecue, like other Southern barbecue styles, consists mainly of pork. Many of the restaurants in the Memphis area will also serve chicken and beef, but chopped pork and ribs are the most popular meats in Memphis-style barbecue.

Ribs cooked in the Memphis style are slow cooked on the pit after they have been seasoned with a rub made up of salt, paprika, cayenne, onion powder, and other spices. The ribs can be served "dry"—right off the pit with no sauce. "Wet" ribs are slathered with a little sauce before serving. Traditionally, Memphis-style barbecue is served without sauce. However, due to tourist demands, many Memphis-style barbecue restaurants will now serve sauce on the side. When sauces are served, they are usually a thinner version of the sweet, tomato-based sauces found in other parts of the country.

Carolina

You might be able to find smoked chicken and other meats in the Carolinas, but for the most part, Carolina barbecue means pork. Whole hogs are smoked with hickory and oak until tender and juicy. The meat is pulled or chopped and served with a tangy barbecue sauce made with a vinegar or mustard base.

In many parts of the country, pulled pork usually refers to meat served in a sandwich. That isn't necessarily the case in the Carolinas. Although pulled pork sandwiches are quite popular, you just as likely to see people eating their pulled pork with a fork.

One of the best example of Carolina-style barbecue is Smiley's Lexington BBQ in Lexington, North Carolina. Smiley's has been around in one form or another for over 60 years. The restaurant, and more importantly the "pit," has changed hands and names several times, but the meat is smoked the same way it always has been. Coarsely chopped or sliced pork shoulder is served with a vinegar-based sauce and traditional sides. There isn't anything fancy about the food, but people come from miles around to give it a try.

Kansas City

Kansas City barbecue is a mixture of a variety of different barbecue cooking styles, but Henry Perry is credited with starting what is now known as the Kansas City barbecue style. Perry was born in a small town outside of Memphis, Tennessee, in 1875. He spent much of his life working in riverboat restaurants as the boats churned up and down the Mississippi and Missouri Rivers.

Later, in 1908, Henry was living in Kansas City and selling barbecue out of a sidewalk stand. For a quarter, workers and passersby could get smoked meats like ribs, beef, possum, woodchuck, and racoon wrapped in newspaper.

ESSENTIAL

Kansas City barbecue sauce is a sweet, tomato-based sauce with a little spice and often times a good dose of molasses.

CHAPTER 2

The Science Behind Smoked Foods

The art of smoking foods is not an exact process like baking. Where normally meats are cooked to a particular temperature, with smoked foods you're cooking to a particular "feel" the meat will have. There is a temperature range that is associated with each "feel," but you can't depend on it being the same each and every time. Learning to recognize the right "look" and "feel" of properly smoked meats is part of the challenge of smoking foods. Understanding the science behind smoked foods will help you to determine what meats look and feel like when they're done.

Why Smoked Foods Taste So Good

Your sense of smell has a lot to do with why smoked foods taste so good. The aroma of smoke sets off a primal feeling in our brain that, for many people, equates to a sense of comfort. When you add seasonings and sauces to those foods, you create a complete aromatic sensation that your brain translates as "this tastes good."

In addition, barbecued and grilled foods taste good because of the people you enjoy them with. Think about the best meal you've ever eaten. It's likely when you reflect on that meal, the reason it was so good involved a combination of good food and great company. Yes, infusing the flavor of smoke into your foods complements most meals, but barbecue is essentially comfort food. And that comfort comes from the memories you are creating by gathering around the smoker, grill, or fire pit with your friends, family, and guests.

Chemical Reactions

Smoked foods taste good for the same reason foods cooked on the stove or in the oven taste good. It's all because of a series of chemical reactions. Certainly knowing the combinations of proteins, herbs, spices, and other ingredients is very important, but without the chemical reactions of the ingredients when heat is applied, you'd just be eating well-seasoned raw food.

Cooked food tastes good, in general, because of a scientific chemical reaction called the Maillard reaction. The Maillard reaction is the technical term for browning. Whether it's the browning on top of a baked loaf of bread or the browning of a steak when it hits the grill, it's the Maillard reaction that transforms the look, feel, and taste of cooked food.

FACT

The Maillard reaction is named after Louis-Camille Maillard, a French chemist and physician who, in 1912, discovered the chemical reaction while trying to recreate biological protein synthesis.

The Maillard reaction occurs when heat, amino acids, and sugars combine to create the browning effect you see in cooked foods. According to

Modernist Cuisine, "The Maillard reaction creates brown pigments in cooked meat in a very specific way: by rearranging amino acids and certain simple sugars, which then arrange themselves in rings and collections of rings that reflect light in such a way as to give the meat a brown color."

The Maillard reaction happens quickly at temperatures between 300°F and 500°F. Barbecue is usually cooked at temperatures below 300°F, but because of the long cooking times when smoking meats, there is enough time to create the chemical reaction necessary for the browning effect to occur.

Layering Flavor

Another reason smoked foods, especially barbecue and grilled foods, taste so good is because the process of cooking adds layers of flavor to the foods. Your taste buds, along with your brain, like to experience different flavors. The taste buds on different parts of your tongue sense flavors uniquely. Here is an example of the different layers of flavor found in a simple pulled-pork sandwich made with smoked pork butt:

- **Layer 1:** The pork butt is loaded with pork fat, and pork fat tastes good.
- **Layer 2:** A rub is then applied onto the surface of the meat. The rub adds salt, sugars, spices, and other ingredients. When combined, they add a layer of flavor on top of the meat.
- **Layer 3:** Smoke and heat is added. The smoke adds the flavor of the wood, while the heat begins the Maillard reaction and changes the taste of the rub.
- **Layer 4:** A sauce or glaze is applied. The sauce or glaze adds another layer that complements the taste from the rub and pork fat.
- **Layer 5:** A toasted bun is used to get the pulled pork to your mouth. Toasting the bun adds a slight nutty taste.

Properly prepared smoked food is actually very complex. When you eat smoked food, your taste buds are able to put all these different layers of flavor together with the help of your brain, and suddenly, you have an appealing flavor combination. Your sense of smell also plays a big part in determining what tastes good. The smell of wood smoke, to most, when combined with the taste on your tongue, creates a unique combination.

Why Pit-Smoked Foods Are So Tender

The need to tenderize cheaper, tougher cuts of meat for many poor people in the South is likely why barbecue became so popular in the United States. At the same time, these techniques were being passed down from generation to generation in other parts of the world.

The desire to make meals that were not only edible, but also tasted good led to the creation of "low-and-slow" barbecue. Tenderizing meats, primarily pork and beef, requires a unique process that many novice pit masters find to be the opposite of what they do in their day-to-day cooking.

A beef brisket, as an example, is one of the most popular cuts of beef to smoke. The brisket is a cut of meat from the breast of a beef. This cut of beef is made up primarily of pectoral muscles. Because a beef doesn't have a collarbone, the pectoral muscles support approximately 60 percent of the total weight of the standing animal. All this work makes these muscles into much tougher cuts of meat.

In order to tenderize a brisket, the connective tissues must be broken down through cooking. Connective tissues typically begin to break down when the internal temperature reaches between 190°F to 200°F. If you cook a brisket to well done at 165°F, you'll have a very leathery piece of meat to contend with. Cook that same brisket to 200°F and it will melt in your mouth.

QUESTION

Why do you call it a "beef" instead of a "cow"?
Technically female cattle are cows and males are called steers. Since you don't always know whether the cut of meat you're eating comes from a female or male, the beef industry refers to the whole animal as a "beef."

Keep in mind, though, you can't cook just any cut of meat to 200°F and have it be edible. Remember, the whole purpose of low-and-slow cooking is to turn the cheaper cuts of meat into something that can be easily eaten. The difference here is the cut of meat. Most cuts of steak, for instance, come from the muscles of the animal that don't work as hard as other parts of the animal. Again, the brisket comes from the chest area of the cow/beef, and since the cow is constantly walking around and spends a lot of time standing up and sitting down, the muscles become stronger, therefore tougher, unlike the filet mignon cut of steak that comes from a part of the cow/beef that does very little work. The lesser working muscle groups don't have as much collagen that needs to be broken down in order to be tender.

ESSENTIAL

The process of tenderizing meat with heat and smoke is similar in nature to braising. Braising is the technique of cooking tough cuts of meat in a liquid at low temperatures for a long period of time. When pit smoking instead of cooking in a braising liquid, the meat is seasoned or rubbed and then it's cooked low-and-slow in its own juices. This process of low-and-slow cooking can make even the toughest of meats tender and moist.

The Time Challenge

The challenge for a lot of backyard pit masters is how much time it takes to smoke larger cuts of meat like a whole brisket or pork shoulder. Many hardcore pit masters will not consider any cooking method other than letting the heat and smoke of the barbecue pit cook the meat. This can be a time-consuming task and certainly isn't for the impatient cook.

For example, an entire brisket can weigh in excess of fifteen pounds, and a pork shoulder can weigh close to that much as well. You should plan, on average, for around ninety minutes of smoking per pound of raw meat. Not every backyard cook has the time or the desire to man a smoker for twenty or more hours, so there are shortcuts that you can use to shorten the cooking times. For example, after approximately four hours on the smoker, meat stops taking on smoke flavor. Therefore, keeping the meat in the smoke is more of a personal cooking preference than a necessity. You could even move the meat to your indoor oven at this point and it won't lessen the smoke flavor all that much.

Additionally, from the minute you place a large cut of meat on the smoker, the temperature rises at a steady rate. At some point, usually around 165°F, the brisket, pork butt, or other cut of meat will reach the point where the internal temperature stops rising. In barbecue circles, this is called "the stall" and is one of the most frustrating aspects of smoking meat. For thirty minutes to over an hour, the internal temperature doesn't increase, and sometimes it may even drop a few degrees. During the stall, it doesn't appear that anything is happening, but in reality a lot is happening inside the meat. This is the part of barbecuing where the tenderizing magic starts.

Muscles have a higher percentage of connective tissues, which is why it takes longer to break them down. Collagen makes up a good portion of the connective tissue, and turning the collagen into gelatin makes the meat tender. This process of breaking down connective tissues and collagen is what makes the final product so tender and juicy.

The breakdown of connective tissues will most likely be finished when the meat's internal temperature reaches 190°F to 210°F. However, the final temperature isn't as important a factor of "doneness" as tenderness. When you use your thermometer probe to check the temperature, you will also use it to check tenderness. When the probe slides into the meat as if it's sliding into butter, your meat is done.

You can speed up the stall and lower the total time it takes to finish smoking the meat by removing the meat from the smoker and double wrapping it in heavy-duty aluminum foil. With the meat wrapped in foil, the remaining cooking time is dependent on heat. Since it's wrapped in the foil, the heat source is not all that important. Wrapping your piece of meat in foil shortens the cooking time the same way a pot of water, on the stove, boils faster with a lid on than it does with the lid off. The meat retains the heat when wrapped in foil. You can leave the foil wrapped meat on the smoker to finish, or bring it into the kitchen and finish in the oven. Either way, wrapping, although frowned upon by barbecue purists, is a good way to ensure your tough cut of meat reaches the temperature needed to tenderize it without you having to tend to your smoker for long periods of time.

Low-and-Slow, Hot-and-Fast, and Grilling

The only differences between smoking foods low-and-slow and hot-and-fast is temperature and time. For both styles of cooking the heat source is still indirect, which means the food being smoked is not directly above the heat source.

Traditionally, barbecue has been cooked at low temperatures, typically in the range of 225°F to 275°F. The exact temperature you use is often dictated by personal preference more than anything else. The lower the cooking temperature, the slower the meat tenderizes. This is where the term "low-and-slow" comes from.

Over the past few years, the way smokers are designed has changed, and pit masters now have the ability to cook with higher temperatures without drying out the meat. Raising the ambient cooking temperature to over 300°F greatly reduces the cooking time. Hotter temperatures and faster cooking times, or "hot-and-fast," is becoming increasingly popular due to busy lifestyles.

As mentioned earlier, grilling is a completely different method of cooking. You could even consider grilling to be the "even hotter-and-faster" method of cooking. While you can still add smoke flavor to your meats while grilling, you won't be able to break down the connective tissues and collagens. This is why when you are grilling, you typically use cuts of meat that don't need to be tenderized, like steaks, chicken, fish, hot dogs, and hamburgers. While grilling is done with direct heat, at the same time, remember that your grill can be used for low-and-slow barbecue when it's set up for indirect heat.

Bark, Smoke Rings, and Raw-Looking Chicken

Chemical reactions play an important role in creating tender, great-tasting smoked foods. They also affect how the meat looks. Because we also use our eyes as part of the eating experience, it is important to understand the different visual terms associated with smoking food.

Bark

Bark is the dark, crunchy layer of flavor that encases most meat that has been on the smoker for an extended period of time. It's called *bark* because it resembles the appearance and texture of tree bark, but it tastes a lot better. For fans of brisket and pulled pork, this jerky-like layer is incredibly appealing. The crunchy texture of the bark complements the tenderness of the meat, while also providing additional bursts of flavor.

The bark is created when the Maillard reaction begins and the top layer of meat starts to dry out. As the water evaporates off the surface of the meat, it creates a crust. The rubs and spices on the meat don't cause the bark to form, but they can help to deepen the bark and make it more flavorful. The creation of bark is not a process that is exclusive to cooking on a smoker or barbecue pit. Bark can form on meat when cooked in the oven as well. However, when combined with smoke, the color of bark deepens from a light brown in color to a deeper mahogany or darker color.

The flavor and texture of bark is so popular that some pit masters try to increase the bark that forms on smoked meats. One technique is to coat meat with ordinary yellow mustard before applying a rub or seasonings. The mustard combines with the sugars, salts, and other ingredients in the rub to create a harder bark. The taste of the mustard disappears as the meat is cooked, leaving behind a rich, dark bark.

The Smoke Ring

The smoke ring is a layer of light red or pink color that you will notice right below the bark when smoked meats are sliced. The interesting thing about a smoke ring is that its creation has absolutely nothing to do with smoke actually penetrating into the meat.

Muscles (cuts of meat) get their color from an iron- and oxygen-binding protein called myoglobin. Myoglobin forms the pigment that makes red meat red. The smoke ring is created when the iron in the myoglobin binds with the carbon monoxide molecules and nitrogin dioxide in the smoke used to add flavor to smoked meats. Chemicals in the meat combine with chemicals in the smoke to provide the appearance of a ring of smoke.

QUESTION

Can I create a smoke ring without using any smoke?
You can create a smoke ring without smoke by increasing the nitrogene dioxide on the surface of your meat. One way to do that is to use a product like Morton's Tender Quick. When heated, the Tender Quick will cause a pink ring on your meat.

But because the smoke ring is such an important part of the barbecue experience, it's an easy way to impress your friends, family, and guests.

As you go through the process of smoking foods, you'll discover that certain woods and different smoking techniques create smoke rings of different colors and depths. It's for this reason that someone who is new to the world of smoked foods should not be too concerned with what their smoke ring does or doesn't look like.

It's Not Raw Chicken, It's Just Pink

There's a reason you'll never see Chicken Tartar on the menu of a restaurant. Eating raw chicken is a definite food no-no. Poultry can be one of the tastiest smoked foods you can serve, but when prepared incorrectly, it can be one of the most dangerous foods you can serve. According to a 2010 *Consumer Reports* investigation, over 66 percent of store-bought chickens were contaminated with salmonella. Ingesting salmonella can cause severe sickness and discomfort.

Most people think pink chicken is just not cooked enough, and although pink chicken can be a sign that it is indeed not cooked enough, properly cooked chicken can be pink, especially around the bones. Pink chicken is prevalent with certain cooking techniques, especially when smoking chicken.

How can you tell if pink chicken is properly cooked? All you need is to learn how to correctly read the internal temperature of the chicken with a good-quality instant-read thermometer. Chicken is done when the breast meat is 165°F and the thigh meat is 180°F.

What happens when you or your guest cut into the chicken and it's pink or maybe even red around the bone? There is a simple test to show the meat is cooked properly. Blot the red area of the chicken with a paper towel. If the paper towel absorbs red liquid, the chicken is undercooked. If the paper towel just looks damp, it's cooked properly.

CHAPTER 3

Smoking Equipment Essentials

The equipment available for smoking food is about as varied as the meal ingredients that find their way into the smoke they produce. Smokers can range from a cardboard box on the back porch to a stainless steel smoker on the kitchen stove or a giant custom-made barbecue pit mounted on a trailer. A common saying in the competition-barbecue circuit is "It isn't the cooker, it's the cook." Don't worry as much about what equipment you are using to cook, because it's really about the process. But it's a good idea to do a little research on the different types of smokers available before picking the right one for your needs.

Types of Smokers

Whatever type of food you are trying to smoke will dictate what kind of smoker you should use. For example, if all you want to do is smoke some salt, you're going to need something different from someone who wants to smoke ten full briskets on a weekend. Not all smokers are created equally. It's important to keep in mind that what you need to smoke food will depend not only on what you plan to smoke but also how often you plan to use the equipment.

Bullet Smokers

It doesn't take more than a glance at this smoker to understand why it's called a bullet smoker. The bullet smoker is also known as a water smoker because of the water pan that is used to control humidity and temperature. Because the water pan sits in the smoker between the heat source and the grates, it also acts as a heat shield to protect the food from burning.

Although there are several makers of bullet-type smokers, the most popular is the Weber Smokey Mountain, or WSM, as it is affectionately called by its millions of users. This smoker has the reputation of being the easiest to use. It is probably as close to a "set it and forget it" cooker as you can find.

The bullet smoker got it's name because of the circular shape and domed lid. Some people thought it had the same shape as a bullet. In the bullet smoker, the heat source is on the bottom with the grate(s) sitting at the top of the cylinder, where the lid is placed. There might be second shelf below the top shelf, but because of the size, the amount of meat you can put on them is limited.

Additionally, the amount of fuel it can hold is limited because of its size, but with an easy access side door, adding fuel is not much of a problem. The fuel source for most bullet smokers is charcoal briquettes, but you can purchase some gas models. The smoke source for charcoal bullet smokers is wood chunks. There are also a couple of bullet smokers that are electric. With gas and electric models, wood chips are recommended.

With a little practice you can cold smoke on a bullet smoker, but it can be a challenge to keep the charcoal lit and the wood smoking at the lower temperatures used in cold smoking. If you're looking for something to smoke pork butts, brisket, ribs, and the like, the bullet smoker is a good choice for both the novice and the experienced pit master.

Kettle Grills

If you're a novice smoker, the kettle grill is the perfect first piece of equipment for you. It's easy to set up, and because of the shape, you can easily learn how to use it for indirect heat cooking, which is vital to good smoked foods.

Although most kettle grills are designed to use charcoal, there are a few gas models, and even an electric version, on the market. When using the charcoal versions, the vents in the lid and bottom make controlling the temperature very simple. With just a little bit of care, a good kettle grill will give you years of enjoyment.

Gas Grills

One of the common mistakes backyard cooks make is thinking that buying a gas grill is an upgrade from the old charcoal grill they had. If you're using the gas grill for cooking a few burgers or steaks, it can be much quicker and easier than a charcoal grill; however, when it comes to smoking food, it is not always the best choice.

The biggest challenge for a gas-grill buyer is finding out which models have features that are good for smoking. The really difficult part is the fact that one feature that is an advantage on one grill can be a disadvantage on another. For example, on some gas grills, the design of the zone heating allows for great heat distribution and you can control the heat very easily. On other grills with multiple heating zones, the design doesn't allow you to have much control at temperatures below 250°F, which you might want to use periodically for smoked foods.

ESSENTIAL

Although many gas grills now come with a smoker box as a standard feature, it's easy to add smoke to a gas grill while cooking if it doesn't have a smoker box already. You can wrap wood chips in a foil packet to make a smoke bomb, or you can buy a cast-iron smoker box that will give you great results.

Ceramic Smokers

The kamado-style cooker has been around for thousands of years. It was popularized in the United States just after World War II and during the Vietnam War when thousands of ceramic-domed smokers were brought home by returning sailors and soldiers who had discovered them in Japan. Although variations have become available recently, most kamado-style cookers are usually made from ceramic. Due to the insulated nature of the materials used to manufacture these grills, they are very efficient with both heat and the amount of fuel needed to create the heat.

Recently, a pellet-burning version of the kamado was introduced into the market, but for the most part, kamado-style cookers are meant to burn lump hardwood charcoal. Although lump charcoal is now readily available almost everywhere, this might be something to consider when deciding if this is the cooker for you.

The biggest drawback to the kamado-style cookers is likely the cost. The cost of a quality kamado-style cooker is a great deal more than a charcoal kettle grill. You will spend as much for a charcoal-fired kamado-style cooker than you will for a high-end gas grill.

Electric Smokers

With an electric box smoker, all you have to do is plug it in, set the thermostat like your kitchen oven, and place your food on the racks. Come back later and you've got smoked foods. It's really almost that simple.

Masterbuilt and Bradley make electric smokers that provide home smokers all the tools they need to create good-tasting smoked foods. You can smoke a brisket or pork butt in the electric box smoker, and you can also produce low-temperature smoke for cold smoking cheeses and other foods that require low heat.

These machines are called *box smokers* because they are shaped like a box; in reality, they look more like small refrigerators, but these smokers, at a cost of around $200, can be an affordable way to get started smoking foods.

Stick Burners

Where other smokers use wood for creating smoke but not to generate cooking heat, a stick burner uses wood for both smoke and heat. For many in the barbecue world, stick burners are the essence of smoked foods. However, as great as they are at helping to create fantastic low-and-slow barbecue, a stick burner isn't as versatile as other smoke-producing tools.

Although some "stick burners" are used with charcoal in addition to wood, the name comes from the burning of wood in the pits. Many stick burners only use wood as both their heat and smoke source. Stick burners require someone to constantly monitor the pit temperature so adjustments can be made, and adding logs every once in a while is still a necessary part of the cooking process.

You can't use a stick burner for cold smoking, so if you're looking for the ability to cold smoke cheeses and other low-temperature foods, a stick burner isn't your best choice. But there isn't a better choice for cooking barbecue in large quantities in a traditional barbecue atmosphere.

Pellet Smokers

Pellet smokers have caused the biggest change in how foods are smoked since the cavemen learned to cook food over an open fire. The combination of electricity with wood pellets has revolutionized the smoker industry.

The pellet smoker is an offshoot of the development and popularity of the home heating systems that use wood pellets for fuel. Pellet smokers may use pellets that are very similar to those used in home heating, but they aren't necessarily the same. Smokers use hardwoods for smoke woods, while wood stoves often use soft woods, like pine, as fuel. It's important to use food-grade pellets in your smoker.

Pellets for smokers provide a variety of options that are not available for stick burners. Wood pellets are available in the more traditional smoke wood flavors like oak, cherry, apple, peach, hickory, and many others, but if you're looking for more exotic tastes, you can now buy pellets flavored with herbs, spices, wine, beer, and many other flavors, making pellet smokers an excellent choice for adventurous smokers.

Also, if you have pellets on hand, it's easy to add smoke to foods using other devices. In many cases, you can use wood pellets in any method that requires the use of wood chips. Pellet smokers provide the ability to use real wood, while you have the luxury of setting the thermostat and walking away, or, if you're planning to cook overnight, getting some sleep (it is completely safe to do this).

Smokehouses

Smokehouses are about as old school as you can get when it comes to smoking meats. The smokehouse is the perfect solution for someone who is interested in smoking hams, sausages, and bacon. A smokehouse is a whole "house" designed for doing nothing but smoking meats, something many backyard cooks dream about. Having a smokehouse was so important to Elvis Presley that he had one built at Graceland.

Traditionally a smokehouse was nothing more than a small building, about the size of a shed, with hooks or another way to hang meat in it. The smoke is generated outside the smokehouse and allowed to draft through the smokehouse. The smoke comes into the smokehouse from the bottom and moves up and through a chimney or vent at the top of the smokehouse. See Appendix B for more information on building a smoke house.

Which Smoker Is Best for You?

Figuring out which type of smoker is best for you is not an easy task. Ask a wood carver how to choose a chisel and he's likely to ask you what you want to carve and what wood you are going to use. Chances are the wood carver has an entire set of chisels. The same is true for the person whose hobby is smoking foods. You're going to need more than one tool.

Starting out by buying two or three different smokers is often not very practical; however, 82 percent of American homes have a grill of some type or another. So the best place to start learning how to smoke foods is by learning how to properly control temperature and smoke output with what you already own.

Using a Gas or Charcoal Grill to Smoke Food

With the right technique, you can use different types of woods to produce smoke on the grill you already have. Over the past several years, grill manufacturers have recognized that adding smoke flavor to foods while grilling is important to consumers, and they've added features that make it easier to generate smoke on a gas grill such as built-in smoker boxes. Several makers have even introduced hybrid grills. These pricey grills will burn propane, charcoal, or wood, which makes it easy for folks to have tasty smoked meals right off their grill. There are, however, simple ways to add smoke flavor even if your grill isn't equipped with the built-in capability to generate smoke.

You've already learned about the differences between direct and indirect cooking. Next you'll learn about the kinds of wood and ways to generate smoke from each of them. If you can generate smoke and produce good smoked foods on your gas or charcoal grill, chances are you can do it on anything.

Wood Dust

Wood dust is a very fine wood powder. It can be used for a variety of different smoking methods, but it is primarily used in cold smoking because it requires very little heat to get it to smolder. Wood dust provides plenty of smoke without providing much heat. It's also used a lot in stovetop smokers.

Wood Chips

Wood chips are one of the easiest wood forms to use when setting up your grill for smoking. You can just toss them directly on the coals for a quick shot of smoke while grilling over direct heat. You can also use wood chips in a smoke bomb or smoker box to provide hours of smoke.

Smoke Bomb

It's easy to make a smoke bomb. First, place one or two cups of wood chips in the center of a double layer of foil. Fold the edges up and over the foil and form it as tightly as possible around the wood chips. After getting as much air as possible out of the packet, crimp all the ends to keep the packet airtight. Take a sharp pencil or a screwdriver and poke two half-inch holes in the top of the packet. You can also create a smoke bomb by placing wood chips in a metal pie plate and covering the whole thing with foil. Poke a hole or two in the top, and you have an easy and inexpensive smoke generator.

Place the smoke bomb as close to the flame as you can get them. If you must, try to move the bars or other parts of the heat-generating mechanisms. You can sacrifice heat for smoke, because you need both to get the job done. It doesn't take a lot of heat to generate smoke with chips or pellets, so chances are you'll be able to find a spot on your grill that will work.

Using a smoke bomb on a charcoal grill is very easy. You can place the smoke bomb directly on the hot coals or on the grill grates. Smoke should start to appear within a minute or two. As soon as the smoke starts to appear, place your food on the grill and close the lid. You can expect about 20 minutes of smoke for each smoke bomb, so plan ahead and have two or three ready for switching out when the smoke stops. Using a gas grill can be a little more of a challenge. You don't want to put the foil-wrapped packet directly on the flame, because it will burn quickly. Getting it as close to the heat as possible to generate smoke and not burning it up takes a little practice.

ESSENTIAL

A simple way to use a smoke bomb on a gas grill without having to worry about the open flame is using an old cast-iron skillet. Preheat the cast-iron skillet and place the smoke bomb in the skillet. Because the cast iron absorbs and retains heat so well, it's a perfect conduit for heating the smoke bomb.

Smoker Box

Wood chips can also be used in a metal smoker box. Because it has a vented lid, a smoker box allows some control of airflow so you can keep the wood chips from bursting into flames. If your grill doesn't come with a built-in smoker box, you can purchase one. Smoker boxes take a lot of abuse from heat and weather, so purchase a good one if that is the direction you decide to go. A cast-iron smoker box will last the longest. Unless your gas grill comes with a smoker box built in, use your smoker box just as you would a smoke bomb.

Smoke, Not Steam

You may have noticed that these methods do not use soaked wood chips. Wet wood does not smoke; it steams. The smoke that is generated doesn't begin until the wood dries out. Using wet wood chips only gives you the illusion that the wood chips are lasting longer than they actually are. The best way to control how fast or slow the chips burn is by restricting airflow.

Soaking the wood only applies when using wood chips for smoke bombs and smoker boxes. When using wood twigs, vines, or skewers, you need to soak them because they burn so quickly, you want to slow that process down. In the case of wood plank grilling, the soaking of the planks allows the wood to burn slowly, releasing a little smoke at a time.

Wood Chunks

Chunks of wood are normally used in smokers that rely on charcoal as their heat source. You can put them in your charcoal grill, directly on the coals, when using indirect heat for cooking. Instead of using a smoke bomb or smoker box to control airflow, the smoker vents are used to keep the temperature low enough to keep the wood chunks smoldering instead of flaming. By opening and closing the vents, you adjust the amount air circulating inside the grill. The vents not only allow you have control over the temperature in the grill or smoker, you are also controlling how fast the wood smokes.

It can be difficult to generate smoke using today's gas grills, especially the infrared-type grills, without a little trial and error or practice. On most medium- to high-end gas grills, you can't even see the flame. Because of this, you have to figure out where to put the wood. Here's where the trial and error comes in. Try setting a chunk of wood directly above the burner; if you have a Weber grill, put the wood chunk on the "flavorizer bars." Keep an eye on the wood. If it catches fire, try wrapping another chunk tightly in foil with a couple of small holes in the foil. This will decrease airflow and allow the wood chunk to smolder without bursting into flames.

If your grill isn't a Weber with flavorizer bars and has some other kind of configuration, you might be able to put the wood chunk directly on the back part of the grill grates. Again, if the wood bursts into flames, limit the amount of oxygen it is getting by wrapping it in foil.

If the grill grates don't get hot enough to cause the wood chunk to smolder, set the wood chunk directly on the burner until it starts to smoke and an ember appears. You can then put the wood chunk on the grates and the heat should keep it smoldering for 30–40 minutes, depending on the size of the wood chunk and how hot your grill is.

Wood Pellets

You can use wood pellets on your gas, electric, or charcoal grill in the same way wood chips are used—in a smoke bomb or smoker box. There are a couple of products on the market for using pellets on grills. The Smoke Daddy and A-Maze-N-Tube smoker are great for generating smoke using pellets (more information in Appendix B).

Twigs and Vines

The next time you trim your fruit trees, grape vines, or berry bushes, save some of the twigs. The best-size twig for smoking would be one that has a diameter similar to a wood pencil. Allow the twigs to sit in the sun for a couple of weeks to dry out.

To smoke with these twigs, you can wrap them in foil to make a smoke bomb and place them directly on the heat source. Or you can soak the twigs or vines in water for an hour and place them directly on the grates over the heat. Place your meat on the top of the twigs or vines and cook just like that. This is a great way to cook meat that doesn't require turning over. Make sure you cover the grill or close the lid when using this method.

Plank Smoking

Plank smoking, or plank grilling, is the technique of cooking food on a piece of hardwood. The plank sits directly on the hot grill grates, and it smolders as the food cooks. The smoke from the plank then infuses a mild smoke flavor into the food. Planks made specifically for grilling are widely available in barbecue supply stores, hardware stores, and even in some grocery stores.

These planks come in a variety of sizes, shapes, and species of wood. Choose a plank size and shape that bests fits the food you want to cook on it. Typically, wood planks come in rectangles or ovals that fit whole salmon fillets, pork tenderloins, or beef steaks. However, there are a variety of other sizes that can be used, depending on ingredients and presentation requirements.

The type of wood used to make a plank will influence the flavor of the smoke and ultimately the food cooked on the plank. There are some natural flavor combinations, like salmon and cedar or pork and apple wood, but don't be afraid to experiment. You can often find a variety package of planks made with different woods. Try them all to see what you like best.

Here are some general guidelines for choosing planks and pairing them with foods:

- **Fish:** The traditional wood for smoking fish, particularly salmon, is cedar. But milder woods like alder and some fruit woods make great pairings, too.
- **Chicken and Pork:** The meat from chicken and pork is a little denser than fish, so it can take the smoke from medium-fragranced woods like maple, apple, peach, and pecan. These woods will leave a nice wood flavor without overpowering the natural flavor of the meat.
- **Beef and Game:** With stronger-flavored meats, you can use stronger woods like oak, hickory, and mesquite without masking the flavor of the meat.

Preparing the Plank

Before cooking, you should soak wood planks for a minimum of thirty minutes, but the longer the better. Some expert plank smokers recommend soaking for as long as several hours. Use the kitchen sink, a dish pan, or just about anything else to submerge the planks in. You can use an unopened can of vegetables or a small, heavy pot as a weight to hold the planks under water.

Soaking the planks is also an opportunity to infuse even more flavor into your meal. Don't limit yourself to soaking the planks in water. Fruit juices and brewed herbal teas are great liquids for soaking planks. The extra layer of flavor will enhance the taste of your meal.

Grilling with a Plank

Although you can use wood planks on charcoal-fired grills, it's much easier to control the temperature on a gas grill; both will require a little bit of practice to learn how to keep the grill hot without burning the plank. Keep a squirt bottle of water handy to put out small fires that may start on your wood plank.

To grill using a plank, preheat your grill to medium-high. Place a clean, presoaked plank on the grill over the heat. Heat the plank until it starts to char and smoke. Either move the wood plank to a cool side of the grill or reduce the heat before placing your food on the plank. Close the lid and smoke until done. If you want a deeper wood smoke flavor, when the plank starts to char on the edges and begins to smoke, flip the plank over before placing your food on it.

Reusing Planks

Wood planks can be reused as long as the char on them has not gone all the way through. Once the wood plank has cooled, wash it in hot water, without soap. If there are pieces of food or excessive char that won't come off, just use steel wool or fine sandpaper once the plank has dried. Allow the planks to dry completely and store them in a dry area.

Building Your Own Smoker

If you search online for "smoke generators," you'll find there are many tools you can buy that are designed specifically for creating smoke, either inside or outside. You can use a smoke generator to build your own smoker, even in a cardboard box. You can cold smoke quite a few foods in a cardboard box, such as cheese, nuts, salt, pepper, and oil. Keep in mind, though, you aren't actually smoking in the cardboard box; you are using the cardboard box as the lid to retain the smoke. Use a smoke generator to create cold smoke, never hot smoke—just let it run with the meat on a rack covered by a cardboard box. Smoke generators are normally electric, so all you have to do is place a rack on a table outdoors, turn the smoke generator on, place a cardboard box over the rack, and insert the smoke generator nozzle through a hole in the cardboard box.

Wok

If you have a wok and an outdoor heat source, like the side burner of a gas grill, you have the ability to smoke just about anything. To do so, line the inside of the wok and the inside of the lid with foil. This will keep the burning wood from scarring the wok and will make cleanup easier.

Place wood dust, wood chips, or wood pellets in the bottom of the wok and cover the wood with a round metal cake rack. Place the meat on the rack and turn the burner on high. As soon as smoke starts to appear, and it won't take long, turn the heat down to low and cover the wok. This method has been used for thousands of years and is a great way to use existing equipment for smoking. Many of today's gas grills have side burners with a rack designed to hold a wok for cooking.

Cast-Iron Skillet/Dutch Oven

You can use a cast-iron skillet or Dutch oven as a smoker. Line the inside and lid of the skillet or Dutch oven with foil. Place wood chips, dust, or pellets in the bottom of the pan and place a rack on top of the wood and the meat on top of the rack. Turn the burner on high, and when it starts to smoke, reduce heat and cover. If your cast-iron skillet doesn't have a lid, you can use heavy-duty foil instead. You can use the Dutch oven on a stovetop in a well-ventilated indoor kitchen or on your charcoal grill or gas grill. The side burner on your gas grill, if equiped with one, is the perfect place to use a Dutch oven for smoking.

Smokerator

Smoke + Refrigerator = Smokerator. If you have an old used refrigerator lying around, you have the basics for a great homemade smoker. All you need to do is cut a small vent in the top of the refrigerator. Typically a 3–4-inch hole is all you need. You can use a reciprocating saw (sawzall) or a large metal hold saw that attaches to your drill. Insert a hot plate in the bottom of the refrigerator and a cast-iron skillet on the hot plate. Heat wood chips or pellets in the cast-iron skillet using the hot plate. When smoke starts, turn the hot plate down a little, and you have an insulated smoker.

Indoor Smokers

You can purchase a variety of stovetop- or oven-smoking tools that allow you to safely smoke foods inside your well-ventilated kitchen. Never use a charcoal, gas, or electric smoker indoors. If it wasn't specifically designed for indoor use, leave it outdoors.

Stovetop Smoker

The stovetop smoker is a simple and safe way to smoke foods indoors on the stove or in the oven. It's basically a metal serving tray with a rack inside and a sliding lid on top. The wood dust or chips are placed in the bottom of the pan with the food rack over the dust or chips. When the pan is heated on the stove, the wood begins to smolder. Placing the food on the rack and closing the lid creates a controlled environment that allows the food to be gently smoked.

Smoke Pistol

The smoke pistol is a nice smoking tool that can be used in the kitchen to generate smoke. It's called a pistol because its shape is somewhat like a pistol. With the barrel, you have the ability to shoot smoke into just about anything you want. Having a tool like a smoke pistol makes it possible to smoke foods that require a very mild smoke or when you want just a wisp of smoke flavor. A smoke pistol works by placing a teaspoon or so of wood dust in the bowl and lighting it on fire. Because it's wood dust, it can be lit with a lighter. They burn for several minutes.

Do It Yourself

You can create your own indoor stovetop smoker with a heavy-duty metal baking dish, a cake rack, and foil. Simply place the wood dust or chips in the bottom of the baking dish with the cake rack inserted into the baking dish, but not directly on top of the wood. Place your food on the cake rack and gently heat the baking pan on the stove until the wood starts to smoke. Reduce the heat to low and cover the entire pan with foil. Seal it tightly, and you've made your own stovetop smoker.

If using any type of smoke-generating tool indoors, it is critical you never use any type of charcoal and that you have a powerful exhaust fan in your kitchen. If at all possible, do your smoking outdoors.

CHAPTER 4

Building and Maintaining Fire and Smoke

Using wood dust or pellets when cold smoking or hot smoking foods on your stovetop doesn't require any type of fire, just heat. As a matter of fact, you don't want a fire at all, really; you just want smoldering wood to generate smoke. However, when smoking outdoors, a fire is a necessity, at least at the beginning of the process. Starting with a proper fire will help to ensure you don't oversmoke your foods or cause a bitter creosote taste.

Types of Fuel

Heat accomplishes two things when used for smoking foods. The first and probably the most important aspect of heat on the grill or smoker is that it cooks the food. Although there are a few foods that taste good raw and lightly smoked, more than likely you're going to want your food cooked before eating it. The second thing heat does is help to generate smoke. Without smoke, the heat in an enclosed grill or smoker is not all that much different than the oven in your kitchen.

There are five basic heat sources you'll find with a grill or smoker; each one has its advantages and disadvantages. And those advantages and disadvantages vary from grill to grill and smoker to smoker, and even from cook to cook.

Gas

Liquid propane and natural gas are the two primary types of gas used to generate heat. Propane is a byproduct of natural gas processing and the refining of petroleum. Propane is a natural gas, but is liquefied to make transportation easier and safer. In addition to barbecues, propane is used for portable stoves, torches, engines, and residential heating. Propane for barbecues is usually sold in five-gallon canisters at gas stations and grocery stores as exchanges. You can also have the canisters refilled at propane stations.

Natural gas is a fossil fuel found deep inside rock formations. Because of how it is transported, the government usually regulates its use. Natural gas is piped directly into homes and businesses. Gas grills and smokers that use natural gas are hooked directly up to the gas system of the house. Keep in mind that most gas grills come from the retailer configured for the use of propane. Because propane burns twice as hot as natural gas, grills need to be reconfigured for the use of natural gas.

Charcoal Briquettes

Charcoal briquettes are made by compressing charcoal, coal, sawdust, a binder, and chemicals like sodium nitrates into a small block shape. If you use the same brand of briquettes all the time, you will be able to rely on a consistent burn time and temperature. Since briquettes have no real flavor of their own, the wood used to generate smoke is able to stand out more. Because of the binders and additives in briquettes, they have far more ash than other types of fuel, which has a tendency to build up and smother the coals.

Lump Charcoal

Lump charcoal is made by cooking hardwoods in a low-oxygen chamber. The process can take several days to burn off the water, methane, and hydrogen from the wood. The end result is pieces of hardwood char that have been reduced by about 25 percent from their original wood state.

Unlike briquettes, hardwood lump charcoal will pass the smoke flavor to your foods. Charcoal doesn't typically smoke, but the lump charcoal manufacturing process leaves little bits of unburned wood inside the lumps. These bits burn and produce smoke, so you get wood smoke flavor without the addition of wood chunks or chips. Some pit masters will supplement the wood flavor by adding additional smoke woods after the fire burns down.

Electricity

Electric smokers and grills are becoming more popular as many apartment complexes are banning any type of cooking equipment that generates an open flame. The advantages of electric smokers like the Bradley or Masterbuilt brands is that they function much along the same lines as an indoor oven, except they generate smoke along with heat.

Wood

Grilling with wood is not as popular for use in the backyard as it is for camping, but you can certainly make a simple wood-burning grill with a couple of bricks and the same grill grates you use on your gas or charcoal grill. Cooking and smoking with wood is the most efficient way to cook if you are looking for smoke flavor. Smoke comes from wood, and since you're cooking with wood, once your fire burns down to ashes, just add another piece of wood or two and you'll get the smoke you want.

Smokers than burn wood are known as stick burners. This is likely the purest form of old school, low-and-slow barbecue cooking. Learning to control the smoke and, more importantly, the temperature inside a wood-burning pit is an art form. You not only have to know the characteristics of your smoker, you have to know how wood burns, how to set up the fire, and how hot and fast the different woods burn, all of which come with practice.

Wood and Smoke Flavors

Not all smoking woods are created equal. Some woods are great for smoking just about any type of food, others are too strong or too mild for some foods. Although this isn't a complete list of woods available for smoking, it will give you a good idea of what woods to use to give you the best tasting results.

- **Alder:** There is a hint of sweetness is this delicate wood. It has been used for centuries as the wood of choice to smoke salmon in the Pacific Northwest. It's perfect for lighter meats like fish, pork, poultry, and some game birds. Alder is the also the perfect wood for cold smoking salmon.
- **Almond:** A semisweet wood with a nutty flavor, almond wood burns with less ash than other woods. It's a great wood for beginners, because fire control is easier. You can also create smoke using the shells from the nuts.
- **Apple:** Apple is one of the most popular smoke woods for pork products. Apple wood–smoked bacon is awesome. The flavor is sweet, and it also works with beef and poultry or for cold smoking cheeses.
- **Apricot:** Use this mild and sweet fruit wood with pork, seafood, and poultry.
- **Ash:** Ash is a fast-burning wood with a medium, distinctive flavor that is great with fish, beef, lamb, or game meats.
- **Avocado:** Avocado wood burns somewhat hot and fast. It has a slightly herbal flavor that's perfect for beef and pork. It's also a good wood to mellow out other stronger-flavored woods.

- **Birch:** This medium-hard wood provides a good amount of slightly sweet smoke that goes well with pork and poultry. Cheeses smoked with birch have a nice rich flavor.
- **Cherry:** Cherry's sweet, fruity flavor makes it one of the most popular smoke woods. Use cherry with everything. A combination of 75 percent cherry with 25 percent hickory or oak makes an unbeatable combination for beef.
- **Chestnut:** It's a little hard to find in the United States, but if you can get chestnut wood, the nutty flavor with a little sweetness is great with almost any meat.
- **Corncobs:** Though not a wood, dried pieces of corncob work quite well in a smoker box or smoke bomb to smoke poultry or fish. Corncobs provide a somewhat sweet flavor that is a little strong. Use a little the first time to see if you like it.
- **Cottonwood:** A softer wood with a very mild flavor, cottonwood is best used as a fuel with other woods to add additional flavor.
- **Crabapple:** Similar to apple wood, crabapple wood provides a lot of rich and fruity smoke that's good with poultry, red meats, game, and lamb.
- **Fig:** This mild and somewhat fruity wood tastes like apple.
- **Grapefruit:** Grapefruit wood is an oily wood so make sure it's seasoned (aged) completely before using. Its natural sweetness combined with a hint of fruitiness is great with beef, pork, or poultry.
- **Grapevines:** Grapevines provide a very aromatic, somewhat tart fruit flavor. It's a great wood for smoking any meat or seafood.
- **Guava:** You can use guava wood with a variety of different meats, but it's especially good on beef and pork. It's similar in flavor to apple with a slightly stronger flowery flavor.
- **Herbal Teas:** You can use herbal teas for cold smoking or in a wok or stovetop smoker. The variety of different flavors makes it easy to mix and match with any meat or seafood. Using herbal teas is a fantastic way to experiment with flavors. Try a lemon-flavored herbal tea with fish or chicken. Apple herbal teas are a perfect match for cuts of pork.
- **Herbs:** When using a wok or stovetop smoker, dried herbs can provide a unique flavor to any meat. Use herbs sparingly, because the

strong flavor can overpower some meats, especially seafood and poultry.

- **Hickory:** The strong, sweet flavor of hickory is great for pork, especially bacon. As one of the most commonly used smoke woods, hickory is also good for smoking ham, beef, or poultry.
- **Kiawe:** This Hawaiian wood is similar to mesquite but somewhat milder. Try it with pork, beef, or fish.
- **Lemon:** Aged lemon wood has a neutral sweetness with a hint of fruitiness. It's a great complement to beef, pork, or poultry.
- **Lilac:** Lilac wood makes a very subtle smoke with slight floral overtones. Use it for cold smoking or smoking seafood and lamb in a stovetop smoker.
- **Lime:** Like other citrus woods, lime should be aged before using. Lime has a light, fruity sweetness that's good with beef, pork, or poultry.
- **Liquor Barrels:** Many liquor companies recycle wood (usually oak) from whiskey and bourbon barrels. The barrel staves soak up the liquor flavor as it ages. The combination of whiskey or bourbon with oak imparts a unique flavor to all meats, but it works best with pork ribs.
- **Manzanita:** Mild manzanita wood burns very hot but yields long-lasting coals. The flavor is similar to hickory and oak, with a little less bitterness. It's good for all meats and vegetables.
- **Maple:** Maple creates a strong smoke with mild, sweet flavors It's a good choice for smoking bacon, and it works well with any poultry or pork. Maple is also a good choice for cold smoking cheeses and nuts.
- **Mesquite:** Mesquite is a small scrub tree that grows in the Southwest. It's very popular in Texas for smoking brisket. Mesquite has a very strong smoke flavor that needs a strong meat like beef. Use caution with this wood—it is very easy to oversmoke this wood.
- **Mulberry:** This is a sweet wood with similar characteristics to apple wood. Use it with beef, poultry, and pork.
- **Nectarine:** Nectarine wood has a mild, sweet flavor. It works well with most meats.

- **Oak, Red:** Red oak is the wood of choice for the famous Santa Maria–style tri-tip. The strong smoke works well with the garlic in Santa Maria dry rubs.

QUESTION

What is Santa Maria Tri-tip?
The tri-tip is a triangular cut of beef from the bottom sirloin. They typically weigh between 1½–2½ pounds. In the 1950s, they became a specialty of the central California town of Santa Maria. The Santa Maria tri-tip is rubbed with salt, pepper, and garlic, and grilled over red oak. The tri-tip gained wide spread popularity after it was featured in the 2004 movie *Sideways*.

- **Oak, White:** A strong, heavy smoke flavor makes this one of the most popular woods for smoking. Try it with beef, pork, or game.
- **Olive:** This fruity wood is perfect for people who like a flavor similar to mesquite without the overpowering smoke flavor.
- **Orange:** Fruity orange wood is an oily wood, so make sure it's seasoned (aged) completely before using. It's great with beef, pork, or poultry.
- **Peach:** Fantastic with most light meats like poultry, seafood, and pork, peach wood smoke has a slightly sweet flavor that mixes well with stronger woods like oak, hickory, or pecan.
- **Pear:** Pear tastes a lot like peach with a little apple mixed in. It's sweet and perfect for poultry, seafood, and pork.
- **Pecan:** If you want a deep golden-brown color on your poultry, pecan wood is the way to go. The flavor is close to hickory, but not quite as strong. You can also use pecan shells as a smoke flavor.
- **Persimmon:** Persimmon provides a medium wood smoke that mixes well with other wood. Use it with pork, beef, or poultry.
- **Plum:** Plum wood's mild, sweet flavor works well with most light meats like poultry, seafood, and pork.
- **Sassafras:** Great with beef and good with pork and poultry, sassafras has a mild, sweet smoke with root beer flavor mixed in.

- **Seaweed:** Head down to the beach and pick up some seaweed. Bring it home, rinse with cold water to remove the salt, and allow it to dry in the sun. The smoke from seaweed adds a spicy flavor that pairs well with clams, lobster, crab, mussels, and other shellfish.
- **Walnut:** Strongly flavored black walnut and English walnut should be mixed with lighter woods. Walnut will overpower poultry and pork, so use this wood with beef or strong game meats.

Not every wood is good for smoking. Don't use pallets, wood from construction sites, or any other leftover wood. Many woods found lying around could have been treated with chemicals that can be harmful when heated. Don't use wood from conifer trees, including pine, fir, redwood, spruce, cypress, or gum trees. Cedar is also a conifer and shouldn't be used for smoking except for plank grilling. Stay away from any old wood you find that is covered with molds and fungi. They may be harmful and will give your food a bitter taste.

What Good Smoke Looks and Tastes Like

One of the biggest challenges for those who are new to smoking foods is figuring out how much smoke is the right amount. Even when smoking a large brisket, just a hint of smoke is all you really need. There's a name for what the proper smoke looks like—"thin blue smoke."

Smoke occurs when there is incomplete combustion. Basically, you get incomplete combustion when there is not enough air to keep a fire burning. Smoke is made up of tiny particles that don't burn. It is mostly soot, tar, oils, and ash. With complete combustion, everything burns, leaving only water and carbon dioxide and ash.

The color of the smoke coming out of your smoker is a key indicator of what your food is going to taste like. Smoke flavor is almost exclusively on the surface of your meat; it doesn't penetrate all that far into the meat. So, if smoke is made up of incompletely burned particles, you want the smallest particles you can get.

Thin blue smoke has the smallest particles. The color is a very pale blue and almost invisible. The particles in white smoke are larger. White smoke can still leave you with a nice smoke flavor, but it can also add bitterness to the meat. Finally, gray smoke has the largest particles and will leave you with a meal that tastes like an old ashtray.

Learning how to get thin blue smoke on a consistent basis takes practice and a little record keeping. One of the most important parts of learning to smoke meats is remembering what previous smoke-cooking attempts were like. A journal, with notes about each smoking attempt, will help to refresh your memory each time you cook. Keeping track of your results will help you to the repeat the correct things you did and make changes to avoid repeating mistakes. Your journal should include the following entries:

- **Date:** The time of year is important, because every smoker functions differently in the winter than it does in the summer, unless it's fully insulated.
- **Quantities:** Record the amount of charcoal you used to start, the weight of the meat, and the amount of wood used for smoke.
- **Times:** Keep track of your times: when you lit the fire, how long it took to get to the proper temperature, when you put the meat on, when you added fuel or wood, and what time the meat was done.
- **Variables:** Keep a list of the injections, marinades, rubs, or sauces you used (or which recipes). Record the type of wood you used for smoke.
- **Notes:** Observations you might have had during the cooking process. Keep track of things like how long it took you to get the right color smoke, how much wind was there, what the meat looks like as you cook it, what it smells like.
- Lastly, **note how the meal was received.** Who liked what and why. Pay close attention to the taste and texture of the meat. If it's good, you're going to not want to guess how you did it.

Taking the time to write everything down will prove to be a valuable exercise for you in the long run.

Tips for Smoking Outdoors

There's nothing quite like sitting outside on a beautiful day, looking up at the sky, and breathing in the delicious smell of smoked foods. Use the following tips to get your outdoor smoking just right.

Locate the Hot and Cold Spots

Every gas grill has areas on the grates that are hotter or colder than other parts of the grill. To properly smoke foods on your gas grill, you have to know where those spots are. When you set up your grill for indirect heat cooking, it will be easier if you already know which spots are cooler than others.

The best way to discover the hot and cold spots on the grill is to bake some biscuits. Preheat the grill to medium, about 300°F. Place two rows of biscuits across the grill from left to right, one row on the back third of the grates and the other on the front third. Close the lid for five minutes and then take a look at the biscuits. You should notice that some of the biscuits are more cooked than others. The spots where the biscuits are less brown than others are where the cooler spots are. The spots where the darker biscuits are the hotter spots. Now you can use this information to set your grill up for proper temperature distribution.

Don't Mess with the Gas

It can be a problem maintaining temperatures lower than 300°F for low-and-slow smoking on some gas grills. Some people have modified their gas grills to achieve these temperatures. Do not attempt to modify your regulator, gas jets, or any other part of the gas assembly. It is not easy, and if done incorrectly, can be extremely dangerous. Liquid propane is highly flammable and explosive if misused.

Clean Your Grill

Whether you're cooking on a gas grill, a charcoal grill, or a smoker, you need to keep the grill clean. All that gunk on the grates, the inside of the grill lid, and on the burners isn't "flavor"—it's gunk. Dried grease, creosote, and everything else that may find its way onto your grill can and will change the flavor of anything you cook on it. If you want to taste the flavor of the wood smoke, you need to clean your grill on a regular basis.

The Minion Method

Jim Minion pioneered a method of generating heat and smoke using the Weber Smokey Mountain, but the method works with a variety of other styles of smokers. The technique can be used to help control temperatures on kettle-type grills and offset and cabinet smokers. The Minion Method is the process of putting several lit charcoal briquettes on top of a stack or pile of unlit charcoal. Use the vents on the grill and smoker to control airflow and keep the temperatures inside the smoker or grill low and stable.

Never Use Lighter Fluid

Don't use lighter fluid to start your charcoal. Charcoal lighter fluids are petroleum-based products that leave a chemical aftertaste even when the smell burns off. Use a charcoal chimney instead. This simple tool consists of a wide metal cylinder with air holes along the bottom and a handle on one side. All you need is a chimney, charcoal, two pieces of newspaper or paper towels, and a tablespoon of cooking oil. Roll one sheet of newspaper into a tube shape and wrap it around the inside of the charcoal chimney bottom. Wad the second sheet of paper up and place it directly in the middle of the chimney bottom. Pour the oil on the wadded up sheet of paper. Dump the charcoal into the chimney and light the paper through one of the holes in the bottom of the chimney. It takes thirty minutes for the charcoal to be ready to use. Once the charcoal is completely hot and ashed over, dump it into your charcoal grill and you're ready to start cooking.

ESSENTIAL

Never light a charcoal chimney on your concrete patio or driveway. Not only will the heat from the chimney discolor your concrete, there is the chance that if there is any moisture in the concrete, it will expand. If the concrete expands too fast with too much moisture, it can explode. Instead light the chimney in the grill.

Start Small

When using wood, briquette, or lump charcoal as your heat source for a low-temperature cook, it's much easier to start with a small fire than a large one. If you want to smoke a pork butt at 235°F, it's much easier to stop at 235°F as the temperature rises than it is to try and cool off the smoker or grill if it rises above the desired temperature.

A common mistake made by novice smokers is using too much smoke. If your food tastes like an old campfire, chances are you used too much smoke. Start out with a little bit of wood and learn how to control the amount of smoke you put on the food.

Dry Wood and a Good Thermometer

Whether you are using wood for heat and smoke or charcoal for heat and wood for smoke, always use dry wood. Wet wood doesn't smoke properly. It will produce a bitter flavor. This rule is primarily for when you are using wood chips to produce smoke. Other woods like twigs, vines, planks, and skewers need to be soaked before using.

Don't depend on the accuracy of the thermometer that comes standard in the lid of your grill. Because it's in the lid the temperature is going to be measured, but you need to know the temperature where the food is located—on the grill grates.

Practice, Practice, Practice

It will take some time to get to know your equipment. Start by learning how to control the temperature on your grill or smoker without any food in it. There's no sense in ruining good meat and vegetables. Once you've learned to keep the temperature stable, you can start to add food. Once you add food, then you can start to learn what wood flavors match the various rubs and sauces you use. Learning to properly smoke foods takes a little time. You won't become an expert without a little practice.

Tips for Smoking Indoors

In some ways, smoking indoors is much like smoking outdoors—the food reacts to the smoke the same as it does on a grill or smoker. However, the techniques and processes you go through to generate smoke indoors are different. Here are a few tips that will help you make good-tasting food in a safe manner.

Leave the Outdoors Outside

Never, ever, use an outdoor grill or smoker indoors. Choosing to do so can be a deadly decision. Burning charcoal produces carbon monoxide—an odorless gas that can kill. Because even small amounts of carbon monoxide can be deadly, it's just not worth the risk.

When you smoke food indoors, make sure you have proper ventilation. Even a little smoke can be dangerous or cause your whole house to smell like smoke for days. It's important to have a properly vented exhaust fan. The fan should vent to the outdoors and not recycle the same air through a filter. Because you're smoking in a small, enclosed stovetop smoker, you don't need as much smoke. Also, wood dust works better than chips when you're smoking foods indoors.

CHAPTER 5

Brines, Injections, Rubs, and Seasonings

How you prepare your food before cooking is one of the most important aspects of the smoking process. Adding brines, rubs, or injections to your food, whether you choose to combine a brine or injection with your choice of rub, is where the magic of smoking starts. Don't limit your use of rubs and brines to meats. You can enhance the flavor of vegetables and seafood with the right brine and rub combination.

Rubs

Rubs serve two purposes when smoking foods. The first, and most important, is the flavor the rub gives your food. Rubs also help create the flavorful crust or bark that you'll find on meats when they come out of the smoker.

Dry rubs are easy to use. Most commercially prepared rubs come in a shaker type bottle. If you're making your own, buy a spice shaker or dredge. You'll find it much easier to apply the dry rub and you'll waste less this way. You want to make sure that you rub the mixture into the fibers of the meat. It's not necessary to rub until your hands hurt—just get the seasoning worked into every little nook and cranny of the meat. This will ensure the dry rub covers every bit of meat.

The sugars used in most rubs, brown or white, are designed to add a counterpoint to the other spices. The caramelization on the surface of the meat from the sugars provides a nice layer of sweetness in the bark.

Brines

Brines are a great way to add moisture and flavor to leaner proteins like pork, poultry, and seafood. Meats can lose as much as 30 percent of their moisture while on the smoker.

The ratio between salt and liquid in a brine is important. When it comes to brines, not all salts are created equal. The two major brands of kosher salt are Morton's and Diamond Crystal. The recipes in this section call for Morton's kosher salt. If you are using Diamond, you need to adjust slightly:

Morton's	Diamond
1¼ teaspoons	1¾ teaspoons

The length of time in a brine depends not only on what you are brining but how it is prepared before brining. A whole chicken, for example, takes longer to brine than a chicken that has been cut into pieces. Use the following chart as a guide for brining times.

▼ **HOW LONG SHOULD I BRINE**

Food	Time
Whole chicken	10–12 hours
Chicken pieces	2 hours
Whole turkey	24 hours
Pork chops	3–4 hours (depending on thickness)
Whole pork loin	18–24 hours
Salmon fillets	8–10 hours
Fish fillets	4–6 hours (1-inch thick or thicker)
	2–4 hours (less than 1-inch thick)
Shrimp	20 minutes

Injections

Injections are used to infuse flavor and moisture into meats. Injections can be used along with brines on pork and poultry, but are typically used instead of brines on cuts of beef.

When injecting meats, use a special syringe that is designed for this method. Place the meat in a casserole dish or pan to catch any liquid that leaks out of the meat. Fill the syringe with the injection liquid and, working in rows, insert the needle into the meat about three-quarters of the way in. While slowly removing the needle, press the syringe plunger, injecting the liquid into to meat. After you've worked your way down one side of the meat, turn it over and repeat.

RECIPES

Basic Brine Mixture

If you're looking to add moisture to your meat, give this basic recipe a try. As you get more comfortable with brining, you can start to add additional ingredients, such as herbs and spices. The most important thing to remember is to keep the salt-to-water ratio the same.

INGREDIENTS | YIELDS ½ GALLON

½ cup kosher salt

½ cup sugar

½ gallon water

Heat water, sugar, and salt in a large saucepan over medium heat, stirring often, until the solids have dissolved, about 10 minutes. Cool to room temperature before brining. See chart in the beginning of this chapter for brining instructions.

How Much Brine Do I Need?

Experience will tell you how much brine you need. This recipe makes enough brine for about 3 pounds of chicken pieces. If you are brining a whole chicken, turkey, or pork roast, you'll need to adjust the recipe to give you enough brining liquid to cover the meat.

Poultry or Pork Brine

There's nothing better than a tender and juicy cut of meat. Try this brine to add some moisture to your poultry or pork.

INGREDIENTS | YIELDS 1 GALLON (ENOUGH FOR 1 WHOLE TURKEY OR 2 PORK SHOULDER BUTTS)

1 gallon water, divided

¾ cup kosher or sea salt

½ tablespoon freshly ground black pepper

½ cup cider vinegar

1 teaspoon allspice

3 tablespoons dark brown sugar

1 teaspoon garlic powder

1 tablespoon onion powder

1 teaspoon dried tarragon

2 teaspoons (or more) crushed red pepper flakes

2 teaspoons dried rosemary

1 teaspoon ground ancho chile powder

1. Bring six cups of water to a boil in a large pot over high heat. Remove from heat and add salt, black pepper, vinegar, allspice, brown sugar, garlic powder, onion powder, tarragon, red pepper flakes, rosemary, and ancho chile powder. Stir gently until ingredients are thoroughly mixed and the salt and sugar are dissolved.

2. Add remaining water to the pot. Cool brine to room temperature, then refrigerate until cold. See chart in the beginning of this chapter for brining instructions.

Brined Foods Cook Faster

Brined foods cook faster, so pay close attention to the internal temperature of your food so you don't overcook anything. In addition to adding flavor to food, brining also adds moisture, but if you overcook your food, all that extra juiciness will be gone.

Lemon-and-Ginger Herbal Tea Brine

Herbal teas are a fantastic way to add interesting and unique flavors to different kinds of meats. This recipe calls for lemon-and-ginger herbal tea, but don't be afraid to experiment with other flavors of tea.

INGREDIENTS | YIELDS 5 CUPS (ENOUGH FOR 3 POUNDS CHICKEN PARTS)

4 lemon-ginger herbal tea bags

4 tablespoons kosher salt

1 cup boiling water

4 cups ice-cold water

2 lemons, quartered

1. In a large bowl, add tea bags and salt to boiling water. Stir until the salt is completely dissolved. Allow to cool for ten minutes.

2. Add cold water and lemon quarters to saltwater mixture. See chart in the beginning of this chapter for brining instructions.

Bourbon Chicken Brine

The bourbon in the recipe adds an additional layer of wood flavor to the meat, from the barrels the bourbon is aged in. Don't worry about alcohol content—between the brining and smoking, the alcohol will burn off, and there won't be anything other than the flavor left.

INGREDIENTS | YIELDS ½ GALLON (ENOUGH FOR 5 POUNDS OF CHICKEN)

2 quarts room-temperature water

9 tablespoons bourbon

¼ cup packed dark-brown sugar

3 tablespoons kosher salt

2 quarts ice water

1 tablespoon black peppercorns

1 tablespoon coriander seeds

3 bay leaves

3 garlic cloves, peeled

1 small onion, quartered

1 small Fuji apple, cored and quartered

1 lemon, quartered

1. In a large pot, combine room-temperature water, bourbon, brown sugar, and salt over high heat. Bring to a boil and stir until solids are dissolved. Remove from heat.

2. Add ice water and remaining ingredients. Cool to room temperature before using. See chart in beginning of this chapter for brining instructions.

Apple Juice Pork Injection

This injection combines the classic flavors of apple and pork, giving you a juicy pork butt perfect for pulling. The sweetness of the apple juice pairs perfectly with the tartness of the vinegar and heat from the cayenne pepper. The orange and lemon juices, besides adding flavor, will help to tenderize the pork as it cooks.

INGREDIENTS | YIELDS 3 CUPS (ENOUGH FOR 1 6–8 POUND PORK BUTT)

2 cups apple juice

2 tablespoons any dry rub (see recipes in this chapter)

2 tablespoons apple cider vinegar

2 tablespoons honey

½ teaspoon cayenne pepper

¼ cup orange juice

½ cup lemon juice

½ teaspoon Worcestershire sauce

2 teaspoons kosher or sea salt

1. In a medium saucepan over medium heat, gently heat the apple juice until it just begins to simmer (about 5 minutes). Reduce heat to low.

2. Add remaining ingredients and stir until all the solids are dissolved and the liquids are combined (about 2 minutes). Remove from heat.

3. Allow to cool completely before using.

Pork Butt Injection

Instead of soaking a pork butt in a brine for hours, you can speed up the flavoring process by injecting the brine directly into the meat. However, you can't just inject any brine—you need a lower-salt injection.

INGREDIENTS | YIELDS 1¾ CUPS (ENOUGH FOR 1 PORK BUTT OR SHOULDER)

¾ cup apple juice

½ cup water

½ cup brown sugar

¼ cup kosher or sea salt

2 tablespoons soy sauce

Gently warm ingredients in a medium saucepan over low heat. Stir constantly until brown sugar and salt are dissolved (about 8 minutes). Remove from heat and cool before injecting.

Cherry Cola Beef Injection

A cola injection adds flavor and sweetness to the meat, and the acids in the cola act as a tenderizer. If you don't have cherry cola, you can use root beer or any other dark soda pop.

INGREDIENTS | YIELDS 2 CUPS (ENOUGH FOR ONE 10–12 POUND BRISKET OR OTHER CUT OF BEEF)

2 cups cherry cola (not diet)

1 tablespoon Texas-Style Dry Rub (see recipe in this chapter)

1. In a medium saucepan, heat the cherry cola until warm over medium heat (about 5 minutes). Add the Texas-Style Dry Rub and stir until dissolved.

2. Remove from heat and allow to cool completely before use.

Cajun Poultry Injection

If you're looking for an injection that will add a lot of flavor to poultry, this recipe is for you. The sweet and salty ingredients add excitement and dimension to every bite.

INGREDIENTS | YIELDS ¾ CUP (ENOUGH FOR 1 10–12 POUND WHOLE TURKEY OR 10 POUNDS OF CHICKEN PARTS)

¼ cup apple cider or juice

1 (12-ounce) bottle beer

3 tablespoons Swimming-in-the-Bay Seasoning (see recipe in this chapter)

2 tablespoons Worcestershire sauce

¾ cup honey

1 tablespoon kosher or sea salt

1 tablespoon ground allspice

½ cup Creole seasoning

¼ teaspoon cayenne pepper

½ cup olive oil

1 teaspoon garlic powder

1. In a small saucepan, heat the apple cider or juice and beer over medium heat for 5–8 minutes, until barely simmering. Remove from heat and add the Swimming-in-the-Bay-Seasoning. Allow the seasoning to steep in the hot liquid for 30 minutes. Strain the solids from the liquid. Allow to cool completely.

2. Pour the beer mixture into a blender along with the remaining ingredients. Blend until combined and smooth.

How to Make a Bouquet Garni

If you don't want to strain the liquid in this recipe, cut a 4-inch square piece of cheesecloth and place the Swimming-in-the-Bay Seasoning in the center. Bring the corners of the cheesecloth together and tie with a string to form a packet. Drop the packet, known as a bouquet garni, into the liquid and steep for 30 minutes. Remove when done preparing the injection. No straining necessary!

Including-the-Kitchen-Sink Dry Rub

This all-purpose dry rub is the perfect combination of citrus and sweet flavors, with just a touch of heat from the chili powder and cayenne pepper. White pepper adds a little tingle on your tongue without being overpowering. Use this rub on just about anything. It's perfect for beef, chicken, and pork, and can be used sparingly on seafood. For a great summer treat, try it on grilled corn on the cob.

INGREDIENTS | YIELDS ½ CUP

1 tablespoon dried lemon zest

1 tablespoon garlic powder

1 tablespoon onion powder

1 tablespoon chili powder

1 tablespoon paprika

½ tablespoon freshly ground black pepper

½ tablespoon cayenne pepper

½ tablespoon white pepper

2 tablespoons brown sugar

2 tablespoons kosher or sea salt

Combine all ingredients in a bowl or jar until thoroughly mixed. Use immediately or keep in an airtight container for up to 30 days.

Mixing Dry Rubs

The easiest way to mix a dry rub is to place all the dry ingredients into a glass or plastic jar and then seal the jar and shake until combined.

Big-and-Bold Beef Dry Rub

Cumin is a traditional dry rub ingredient for barbecuing. It adds an aromatic layer of smoky flavor to the meat in addition to what you get from the actual smoke. Layer this rub on a beef brisket or tri-tip roast with a heavy hand. In addition to great flavor, the rub will give the meat a nice dark "bark."

INGREDIENTS | YIELDS 1¼ CUPS

1 cup ancho chile powder

1 tablespoon ground cumin

1 tablespoon dried coriander

1 teaspoon cayenne pepper

2 teaspoons dry mustard

2 teaspoons dried oregano

1 tablespoon kosher or sea salt

1 teaspoon freshly ground black pepper

Combine all ingredients in a bowl or jar until thoroughly mixed. Use immediately or keep in an airtight container for up to 30 days.

Chili or Chile Powder

"Chili" powder is a mixture of ground chilies and other ingredients including cumin, salt, and pepper. "Chile" powder refers to ground chilies (typically one type of chile), with no additional ingredients.

Taste of Caribbean Dry Rub

The addition of allspice gives this dry rub a unique flavor that is native to the islands of the Caribbean.

INGREDIENTS | YIELDS ¼ CUP

1 tablespoon brown sugar

2 teaspoons allspice

2 teaspoons onion powder

½ teaspoon dried thyme

1 teaspoon kosher or sea salt

½ teaspoon nutmeg

Combine all ingredients in a bowl or jar until thoroughly mixed. Use immediately or keep in an airtight container for up to 30 days.

Sweet Rub

The sugars used in most rubs, brown or white, are designed to add a counterpoint to the other spices. The caramelization on the surface of the meat from the sugars provides a nice layer of sweetness in the bark.

Sprinkle Dry Rub

Sprinkle this spicy dry rub on beef and pork. For seafood and poultry, sprinkle it on a little lighter.

INGREDIENTS | YIELDS ½ CUP

2 tablespoons freshly ground black pepper

6 tablespoons kosher or sea salt

1½ tablespoons garlic powder

1 tablespoon cayenne pepper

3 tablespoons chili powder

4 tablespoons paprika

Combine all ingredients in a bowl or jar until thoroughly mixed. Use immediately or keep in an airtight container for up to 30 days.

Winner, Winner, Chicken Dinner Dry Rub

Dry mustard adds a nice sharp spice flavor to this rub without adding heat, which makes it perfect for chicken and other poultry. For a little more kick, use a smoked or hot paprika.

INGREDIENTS | YIELDS ½ CUP

6 tablespoons kosher or sea salt

2 tablespoons dry mustard

1 tablespoon paprika

2 tablespoons MSG (monosodium glutamate)

3 tablespoons freshly ground black pepper

2 tablespoons garlic powder

Combine all ingredients in a bowl or jar until thoroughly mixed. Use immediately or keep in an airtight container for up to 30 days.

Use of MSG

Some people have short-term reactions to MSG, including headaches and nausea. If you have health concerns about MSG in this or any other dry rub, just omit it. The flavor won't pop quite as much, but it will still have plenty of flavor.

Kansas City–Style Dry Rub

Kansas City–style barbecue is known for being sweet with just a touch of heat. Don't be afraid to experiment with the level of cayenne pepper or chili powder in this recipe. You can also use chipotle or serrano chili powder instead of the cayenne.

INGREDIENTS | YIELDS 2½ CUPS

2 cups sugar

¼ cup paprika

2 teaspoons chili powder

½ teaspoon cayenne

½ cup kosher or sea salt

2 teaspoons freshly ground black pepper

1 teaspoon garlic powder

Combine all ingredients in a bowl or jar until thoroughly mixed. Use immediately or keep in an airtight container for up to 30 days.

No Clumping

Rubs with a lot of sugar in them have a tendency to clump, especially in humid climates. To help keep clumping to a minimum, place a saltine cracker or two in your rub container. The cracker will absorb the moisture before your rub does.

Memphis-Style Dry Rub

Memphis dry rubs give pork ribs a robust flavor. This means you won't need a sauce to go with the meat once smoked. However, if you'd like to add a sauce to your ribs, try Sweet and Sassy Memphis-Style Barbecue Sauce in Chapter 6. Wait until the ribs are done and off the smoker before saucing them.

INGREDIENTS | YIELDS ½ CUP (ENOUGH FOR 2 RACKS OF RIBS)

2 tablespoons paprika

1 tablespoon freshly ground black pepper

1 tablespoon dark brown sugar

1½ teaspoons kosher or sea salt

1 teaspoon celery salt

1 teaspoon garlic powder

1 teaspoon dry mustard

1 teaspoon cumin

¼ teaspoon cayenne pepper

Combine all ingredients in a bowl or jar until thoroughly mixed. Use immediately or keep in an airtight container for up to 30 days.

Texas-Style Dry Rub

With its layers of hot and sweet flavors, this dry rub recipe is a Texas-style barbecue staple. Texas-style barbecue, especially brisket, is served with sauce on the side, if it's served at all. Use the Texas Table Sauce in Chapter 6 if you need a sauce.

INGREDIENTS | YIELDS 1½ CUPS (ENOUGH FOR 2 LARGE BRISKETS)

¼ cup kosher or sea salt

½ cup light brown sugar

2 tablespoons freshly ground black pepper

2 tablespoons ground cumin

1 tablespoon dry mustard

1 teaspoon cayenne pepper

½ teaspoon ground chipotle powder

Combine all ingredients in a bowl or jar until thoroughly mixed. Use immediately or keep in an airtight container for up to 30 days.

Carolina-Style Dry Rub

Carolina barbecue essentially means pulled pork, and pulled pork means using a pork butt or pork shoulder. For a truly authentic Carolina barbecue meal, serve pulled pork sandwiches topped with the Tangy and Creamy Cole Slaw (see recipe in Chapter 11).

INGREDIENTS | YIELDS ½ CUP (ENOUGH FOR A 5–6 POUND BOSTON BUTT)

1 tablespoon mild paprika

2 teaspoons light brown sugar

1½ teaspoons hot paprika

½ teaspoon celery salt

½ teaspoon garlic salt

½ teaspoon dry mustard

½ teaspoon freshly ground black pepper

½ teaspoon onion powder

¼ teaspoon kosher or sea salt

Combine all ingredients in a bowl or jar until thoroughly mixed. Use immediately or keep in an airtight container for up to 30 days.

Tamed Cajun Seasoning

If you love the flavor of Cajun food but are a little timid when it comes to spiciness, this is the recipe for you. This mixture can be used as a barbecue dry rub, but it also makes a fantastic all-purpose seasoning. If you want to try a slightly spicier rub, add a little cayenne pepper.

INGREDIENTS | YIELDS ½ CUP

3 tablespoons paprika

2 tablespoons kosher or sea salt

2 tablespoons dried parsley

2 teaspoons onion powder

2 teaspoons garlic powder

1 teaspoon freshly ground black pepper

1 teaspoon dried oregano

1 teaspoon dried basil

1 teaspoon dried thyme

½ teaspoon celery salt

Combine all ingredients in a bowl or jar until thoroughly mixed. Use immediately or keep in an airtight container for up to 30 days.

Swimming-in-the-Bay Seasoning

This seasoning mix is all about big and bold flavors. Use as little or as much as you prefer, depending on how you like your seafood. Make sure you use sweet Hungarian paprika and not the hot version!

INGREDIENTS | YIELDS ¼ CUP

1 teaspoon cayenne pepper

1 teaspoon ground celery seed

1 teaspoon sweet Hungarian paprika

1 teaspoon dry mustard

1 teaspoon ground black pepper

1 teaspoon ground bay leaf

¼ teaspoon ground allspice

¼ teaspoon ground ginger

¼ teaspoon grated nutmeg

¼ teaspoon ground cardamom

¼ teaspoon ground cinnamon

Combine all ingredients in a bowl or jar until thoroughly mixed. Use immediately or keep in an airtight container for up to 30 days.

Santa Maria Seasoning

This is the seasoning that made the tri-tip famous. The California town of Santa Maria took a throwaway cut of meat and turned it a popular California cusine. After seasoning the tri-tip, it's grilled over red oak.

INGREDIENTS | YIELDS ¼ CUP

1 teaspoon salt

1½ teaspoons garlic salt

½ teaspoon celery salt

¼ teaspoon ground black pepper

¼ teaspoon onion powder

¼ teaspoon paprika

¼ teaspoon dried dill

¼ teaspoon dried sage

¼ teaspoon crushed dried rosemary

Combine all ingredients in a bowl or jar until thoroughly mixed. Use immediately or keep in an airtight container for up to 30 days.

Smoked Olive Oil

Smoked oils are an easy way to add a little smokiness to foods without breaking out all the smoking equipment. Sauté some onions and peppers in smoked oil and you'll be amazed at the additional flavor it adds. This oil will keep for about a month in a tightly sealed, dark-colored container.

INGREDIENTS | YIELDS 2 CUPS

2 cups extra-virgin olive oil

2 sprigs rosemary (or any other herb)

1 tablespoon whole peppercorns

Clean Oil Is Good Oil

Use the best quality extra-virgin olive oil you can afford. This will help to ensure that any impurities, which cause the oil to go bad, have been filtered out. After you're done smoking the oil, it's a good idea to strain out any solids you've put in during the smoking process. You can leave them in for appearance sake, but removing them will help the high-quality flavor last longer.

1. Set up smoker or grill for indirect cooking. Preheat for low-temperature cooking. Place a smoke bomb or smoker box with 2 cups of wood chips on the heat source. (See Chapter 3 for instructions on making a smoke bomb.)

2. Pour the olive oil into a shallow plate or casserole dish. Place one rosemary sprig at each end of the pan. Evenly distribute the peppercorns throughout the oil.

3. Place oil on grill grates as far away from heat as possible. Close lid and smoke for 3–4 hours, stirring every 20 minutes. The oil will darken as it absorbs the smoke. Taste after 3 hours to determine if you want more smoke. You can smoke for as long as you like.

Smoked Salt

Smoked salt is a fantastic replacement for regular salt in just about any dish. A dash or two on your eggs in the morning will remind you of a campfire breakfast. If the flavor is too strong after smoking, just mix it with a little unsmoked salt until you get the flavor you want.

INGREDIENTS | YIELDS 2 CUPS

2 cups kosher or sea salt, the coarser the better

1. Set up smoker or grill for indirect cooking. Preheat for low-temperature cooking. Place a smoke bomb or smoker box with 2 cups of wood chips on the heat source. (See instructions in Chapter 3 for making a smoke bomb.)

2. Place salt in a disposable foil pie pan in a thin layer. Place on grill and smoke for 1 hour. Check smoke flavor and smoke longer if you want a stronger flavor. Cool salt and store in a sealed jar.

Smoked Peppercorns

Smoked peppercorns add amazing flavors to a wide range of dishes. Try smoking different types of peppercorns for flavors to match regional and international dishes.

INGREDIENTS | YIELDS 1 CUP

1 cup Tellicherry black peppercorns, cracked into large pieces

Cold smoke the peppercorns for 4 hours using a strong wood smoke like oak or mesquite. Store peppercorns in a tightly sealed container.

Cracking Peppercorns

The easiest way to crack peppercorns is to place them on a heavy-duty wooden cutting board and hit them once or twice with the bottom of a heavy skillet or pan.

CHAPTER 6

Barbecue Sauces, Mops, and Glazes

Sauces, mops, and glazes should complement the smoke flavor and seasonings you used instead of covering up all the hard work you did in preparing your smoked foods. Although sauces, glazes, and mops are often used for the same purpose when smoking foods, they all serve different purposes. Sauces are served on the side, while glazes are applied while the meat is cooking. So, a barbecue sauce should be served on the side, but when applied during cooking it's a glaze. Mops are thin, watery mixtures applied during cooking to increase moisture and flavor while cooking.

Barbecue Sauces

Barbecue sauces may just be one of the most abused condiments in the smoked food or barbecue world. In the early days of smoked foods, barbecue sauce was served as a table sauce, meaning it was added to the food at the table. Using barbecue sauce at the table allows your guests to control the amount of sauce they use. Heavy use of barbecue sauce covers up your flavor.

Mops

Mops are thin basting liquids used to infuse flavor in smoked meats while also providing additional moisture. The term "mop" comes from the 1960s, when famed Texas pit master Walter Jetton used a real mop to apply his basting sauce to meats being cooked over large open pits in the ground. Mops are typically acidic and very thin.

Glazes

A barbecue glaze is applied toward the end of the smoking process to add just a little additional flavor. You can use any of the sauce recipes in this chapter to glaze your meat. But a glaze is different than a sauce. You can use a barbecue sauce as a glaze, but you shouldn't use a glaze as a sauce.

RECELES

Texas-Style Barbecue Sauce

The bold flavors of this sauce match perfectly with beef. Use it with Texas-Style Dry Rub (see recipe in Chapter 5) on a brisket for the taste of a genuine Texas barbecue. Serve the meat on sheets of butcher paper with the sauce on the side, just like you'd find in some of the most popular Texas barbecue joints.

INGREDIENTS | YIELDS 2 CUPS

½ cup unsalted butter
3 cloves garlic, minced
1 medium onion, chopped
½ cup Worcestershire sauce
1 cup vinegar
1 cup vegetable oil
½ cup beer
3 tablespoons lemon juice
1 tablespoon hot sauce
½ cup honey
1 teaspoon freshly ground black pepper
1 teaspoon onion salt
1 teaspoon garlic salt

1. In a medium saucepan, bring all ingredients to a boil over medium-high heat, stirring occasionally.

2. When the sauce reaches a boil, reduce heat to low and simmer for 20 minutes.

3. Use an immersion blender to purée the sauce until smooth. If you don't have an immersion blender, allow the sauce to cool slightly and transfer to a blender to purée.

4. Allow to cool to room temperature. Use immediately or refrigerate in a sealed container for up to 30 days.

Texas Table Sauce

Texas is big enough to have several regional barbecue styles all their own. This Texas table sauce is representative of the Central Texas style of barbecue. In the Texas tradition, this sauce is served alongside beef, sausage, and even pork. Don't forget to toss a couple slices of white bread on the plate to mop up the juices.

INGREDIENTS | YIELDS 3 CUPS

½ cup ketchup

¼ cup chili sauce

1 cup butter

3 tablespoons Worcestershire sauce

1 clove garlic, pressed

2 tablespoons minced onion

¾ cup apple cider vinegar

¾ cup warm water

1 tablespoon kosher or sea salt

1 teaspoon coarsely ground black pepper

1 teaspoon sweet or hot Hungarian ground paprika

1 tablespoon dark brown sugar

1 tablespoon dark molasses

3 tablespoons dry mustard

1. In a medium saucepan, combine, ketchup, chili sauce, butter, Worcestershire sauce, garlic, onion, vinegar, and water over low heat.

2. Stir in salt, pepper, paprika, brown sugar, molasses, and mustard. Bring to a boil.

3. Reduce heat and simmer over low heat, uncovered, for 1 hour. Remove from heat and allow to cool to room temperature. Use immediately or refrigerate in a sealed container for up to 30 days.

Storing Your Barbecue Sauce

Used ketchup squeeze bottles are a fantastic and inexpensive way to store your homemade barbecue sauces. Wash them out completely with hot soapy water, allow to dry, and then fill them with your sauces.

Sweet and Sassy Memphis-Style Barbecue Sauce

Memphis-style barbecue starts out sweet and ends with some sassy heat, thanks to some yellow mustard and black pepper. If you want to cut down a little on the spice, reduce the amount of black pepper and red pepper flakes. Serve this sauce as a table sauce for pulled pork. It's also perfect for ribs. Just lightly coat ribs 15 minutes before removing them from the smoker or grill.

INGREDIENTS | YIELDS 2½ CUPS

2 cups ketchup

½ cup yellow mustard

½ cup dark brown sugar

¼ cup apple cider vinegar

3 tablespoons Worcestershire sauce

1 tablespoon onion powder

1 tablespoon chili powder

1 tablespoon freshly ground black pepper

2 teaspoons garlic powder

1 teaspoon crushed red pepper flakes

½ teaspoon celery salt

½ teaspoon kosher or sea salt

1. Combine all of the ingredients in a nonreactive medium saucepan. Whisk or use an immersion blender to combine and remove any lumps you find.

2. Bring to a low boil over medium heat, stirring frequently to keep from burning. Reduce heat to low and simmer for 20 minutes to thicken the sauce.

3. Remove from the heat and allow to cool to room temperature. Use immediately or refrigerate in a sealed container for up to 30 days.

Nonreactive Pans

A nonreactive pan is one that is non-pourous and does not produce a chemical reaction when it comes into contact with acidic foods.

Kansas City–Style Barbecue Sauce

Kansas City–style sauce has a rich flavor and lots of sweetness. The combination of ketchup, brown sugar, molasses, and vinegar provides the perfect mixture of sweet and tangy. Due to the amount of sugar in this sauce, apply it to the meat shortly before removing from the smoker or grill to keep it from burning.

INGREDIENTS | YIELDS 2½ CUPS

2 tablespoons unsalted butter

1 small yellow onion, peeled and finely chopped

3 cloves garlic, minced

2 cups ketchup

⅓ cup molasses

⅓ cup dark brown sugar

⅓ cup apple cider vinegar

2 tablespoons yellow mustard

1 tablespoon chili powder

1 teaspoon freshly ground black pepper

½ teaspoon cayenne pepper

Cayenne Pepper Substitutes

Some people love the heat cayenne pepper provides to foods, but don't like the harsh flavor. You can substitute with cayenne pepper sauce (which isn't as harsh in flavor), red pepper flakes, or hot paprika.

1. Melt butter in a medium saucepan over medium heat. Add the onion and cook, stirring gently, until onion is translucent (about 4 minutes). Add garlic and cook for another minute.

2. Add remaining ingredients to saucepan and stir to combine. Bring to a low boil, stirring frequently. Reduce heat to low and simmer for 30 minutes or until thickened slightly.

3. Use an immersion blender to purée the sauce until smooth. If you don't have an immersion blender, allow the sauce to cool slightly and transfer to a blender to purée. Use immediately or refrigerate in a sealed container for up to 30 days.

Carolina Pulled Pork Vinegar Sauce

Carolina sauces like this one are thin, watery, and vinegar based. The brown sugar and red pepper flakes cut some of the vinegar tanginess. This sauce can be an acquired taste for many barbecue enthusiasts.

INGREDIENTS | YIELDS 2 CUPS

1½ cups apple cider vinegar

½ cup ketchup

2 tablespoons yellow mustard

2 tablespoons brown sugar

1 teaspoon freshly ground black pepper

1 teaspoon kosher or sea salt

½ teaspoon crushed red pepper flakes

1. Combine all ingredients in a medium saucepan over low heat, stirring until all ingredients dissolve. Simmer for 5 minutes.

2. Remove from heat and serve warm as a table sauce. This sauce will keep almost indefinitely stored in an airtight container in the refrigerator.

Carolina Mustard Sauce

This sauce has a completely different flavor from what you'll find in most parts of the country. It's quite tart with just a little sweetness and works well with smoked pork. A little of this sauce goes a long way, so be careful the first time you give it a try.

INGREDIENTS | YIELDS 1½ CUPS

¾ cup yellow mustard

¾ cup apple cider vinegar

¼ cup sugar

1½ tablespoons unsalted butter

2 teaspoons kosher or sea salt

½ teaspoon Worcestershire sauce

1¼ teaspoons freshly ground black pepper

½ teaspoon crushed red pepper flakes

1. In a medium saucepan, combine all ingredients, stirring to blend. Simmer over low heat for 30 minutes.

2. Let stand at room temperature for 1 hour before using. Refrigerate leftovers in a sealed container for up to 30 days.

Alabama White Barbecue Sauce

Mayonnaise-based barbecue sauce is one of the hidden gems of the smoked foods culture. It's not found in too many places outside of northern Alabama. It was made famous by one of the kings of Southern barbecue, Big Bob Gibson. His son-in-law, Chris Lilly, carries on the family's barbecue traditions as one of the most successful pit masters on the competition barbecue circuit today.

INGREDIENTS | YIELDS 2 CUPS

2 cups mayonnaise

1½ tablespoons kosher or sea salt

2 tablespoons freshly ground black pepper

6 tablespoons white vinegar

6 tablespoons lemon juice

4 tablespoons sugar

Combine all ingredients in a medium bowl. Use immediately or refrigerate in a sealed container for up to 2 weeks.

Dunk Your Chicken

Traditional Alabama white barbecue sauce is served on chicken. Large containers of sauce are made and whole chickens are dunked in the sauce before being put on the smoker. You can do the same thing with pieces if you want. However, if you use this technique, discard any leftover sauce that has had raw chicken dunked in it.

Horseradish Barbecue Sauce

This sauce will make a great addition to just about any smoked beef dish. Horseradish has an intense spicy flavor that is different from the hot and spicy flavor you get from chili peppers.

INGREDIENTS | YIELDS 2 CUPS

1 cup unsalted butter
Juice of 2 large lemons
½ cup apple cider vinegar
½ cup ketchup
2 teaspoons Worcestershire sauce
3 drops hot sauce
2 tablespoons freshly grated horseradish
¼ teaspoon kosher or sea salt
¼ teaspoon freshly ground black pepper

1. In a medium saucepan, melt the butter over low heat.

2. Stir in the remaining ingredients. Heat gently and continue stirring until combined, about 10 minutes.

3. Allow to cool to room temperature. Use immediately or refrigerate in a sealed container for up to 30 days.

Easy-Peasy Quick Barbecue Sauce

Ketchup is the mother of all sauces for barbecue. If you have ketchup and two other ingredients, you've got the makings of a decent sauce. Add a different twist to your sauce by using something like jalapeño ketchup or balsamic vinegar ketchup.

INGREDIENTS | YIELDS 1 CUP

1 cup ketchup
2 tablespoons sugar
3 tablespoons vinegar
2 tablespoons Worcestershire sauce
4 tablespoons minced shallots
1 dash Tabasco sauce

Mix all ingredients together in a small saucepan over medium-high heat. Bring to a boil, then reduce heat to low. Simmer sauce for 10 minutes until reduced slightly. Keep for up to 14 days in a sealed container in the refrigerator.

Apple-Piggy Barbecue Sauce

This sauce is ideal for juicy pork spare ribs. The sweetness of the apple jelly along with the tang of the vinegar provides a sweet-and-sour taste. And the chili powder adds a little heat.

INGREDIENTS | YIELDS 3¼ CUP

2 cups apple jelly

1 cup ketchup

¼ cup brown sugar

1 tablespoon apple cider vinegar

1 tablespoon chili powder (or to taste)

Mix all ingredients together in a small saucepan over medium-high heat. Bring to a boil, then reduce heat to low. Simmer sauce for 10 minutes until reduced slightly. Keep for up to 30 days in a sealed container in the refrigerator.

Cola Barbecue Sauce

The sweetness of cola provides a deep caramelized flavor when used for grilling and complements most meats very well. You can mix this up a little by using root beer instead of cola or regular ketchup instead of balsamic vinegar ketchup. You could also use soy sauce instead of Worcestershire sauce.

INGREDIENTS | YIELDS 2 CUPS

1 cup balsamic vinegar ketchup

2 cups cola (not diet)

1 teaspoon garlic powder

1 teaspoon Worcestershire sauce

Mix all ingredients together in a small saucepan over medium-high heat. Bring to a boil, then reduce heat to low. Simmer sauce for 10 minutes until reduced slightly. Keep for up to 30 days in a sealed container in the refrigerator.

Tweak-Your-Own Barbecue Sauce

Chances are, you already have a jar of barbecue sauce in your pantry. And you probably also have some type of fruit jelly, marmalade, or preserves. Mix them together for a sweet and tasty sauce that goes with just about anything. For a little extra kick, try a pepper jelly combined with a honey barbecue sauce.

INGREDIENTS | YIELDS 2 CUPS

1 cup store-bought tomato-based barbecue sauce

1 cup any fruit jelly, marmalade, or preserves

Pour barbecue sauce and jelly into a small saucepan. Cook and stir over low heat until the jelly, marmalade, or preserves has melted and is fully incorporated into the barbecue sauce. Use immediately or refrigerate in a sealed container for up to 2 weeks.

Texas Barbecue Mop Sauce

This mop has all the flavors that have made Texas barbecue one of the most popular styles of barbecue there is. The big, bold flavors match perfectly with Texas-Style Dry Rub (see recipe in Chapter 5) and the Texas-Style Barbecue Sauce (see recipe in this chapter).

INGREDIENTS | YIELDS 1½ CUPS (ENOUGH FOR 1 LARGE WHOLE BRISKET)

1 cup cider vinegar

½ cup water

1 tablespoon Worcestershire sauce

1 tablespoon coarsely ground black pepper

1 tablespoon kosher or sea salt

2 teaspoons vegetable oil

½ teaspoon cayenne pepper

Combine all ingredients in a medium bowl. Whisk or blend together. Use immediately or refrigerate in a sealed container for up to 30 days.

If You're Looking, You're Not Cooking

Mops typically are applied every 60 to 90 minutes during the smoking process. Any more often than that and the constant opening and closing of the smoker door will cause temperature fluctuations, and your meat will take too long to cook.

Pork Rib Mop

Ribs are one of the best meats to mop. A mop is a great way to add flavor to ribs without turning them to mush.

INGREDIENTS | YIELDS ½ CUP (ENOUGH FOR 2 RACKS OF PORK RIBS)

½ cup apple cider vinegar

2 tablespoons Dijon mustard

2 tablespoons fresh lemon juice

½ teaspoon Worcestershire sauce

Combine all ingredients in a small bowl and whisk until combined. Use immediately or refrigerate in a sealed container for up to 30 days.

Easy Chicken Mop Sauce

Using a store-bought or homemade sauce as the base for your mop is a great way to get started creating your own flavor profiles. Using different barbecue sauces and mixing them with different beers will provide plenty of combinations. Use flavored vinegars or smoked salts for even more variety.

INGREDIENTS | YIELDS 2 CUPS (ENOUGH FOR 2 OR 3 WHOLE CHICKENS)

1 cup apple cider vinegar

½ cup beer

½ cup barbecue sauce, store-bought or homemade

1½ teaspoons kosher or sea salt

1½ teaspoons freshly ground black pepper

2 tablespoons hot sauce

Combine all ingredients in a small bowl and whisk until combined. Use immediately or refrigerate in a sealed container for up to 30 days.

Mop-Anything Mop Sauce

This simple, easy-to-make mop sauce tastes great on chicken, pork, or beef. You can change up the flavors by simply changing the dry rub you use.

INGREDIENTS | YIELDS 1 CUP

½ cup cider vinegar

½ cup apple juice

1 tablespoon kosher or sea salt

2 tablespoons any dry rub (see recipes in Chapter 5)

Combine all ingredients in a small bowl and whisk until combined. Use immediately or refrigerate in a sealed container for up to 30 days.

Vinegar

Most barbecue recipes call for apple cider vinegar, but you don't have to limit yourself to just one type. There are a variety of different vinegar flavors. Try rice wine vinegar for a milder flavor or a fruit-flavored one for sweetness.

Perfect Pork Mop Sauce

Use this mop to add a little additional flavor and moisture as you smoke pork butts for pulled pork or racks of pork ribs. The white vinegar has a slightly milder flavor than apple cider vinegar, but it adds just enough tang without being overpowering.

INGREDIENTS | YIELDS 3 CUPS (ENOUGH FOR 2 OR 3 PORK SHOULDER BUTTS OR RACKS OF RIBS)

1 cup white vinegar

1 cup water

1 cup beer

¼ cup Worcestershire sauce

2 tablespoons any dry rub (see recipes in Chapter 5)

1 tablespoon brown sugar

½ tablespoon kosher or sea salt

½ tablespoon garlic powder

1 teaspoon cayenne pepper

In a small saucepan, combine all ingredients and gently warm over low heat, stirring until the sugar is dissolved. Use immediately or refrigerate in a sealed container for up to 30 days.

Brown-Sugar Salmon Glaze

Brown sugar is really just white sugar mixed with molasses. It adds a delicious sweetness to all your smoked food favorites.

INGREDIENTS | YIELDS 4 TABLESPOONS (ENOUGH FOR 2 POUNDS OF SALMON)

1 tablespoon brown sugar

2 teaspoons unsalted butter

1 teaspoon honey

1 tablespoon olive oil

1 tablespoon Dijon mustard

1 tablespoon soy sauce

¾ teaspoon kosher or sea salt

¼ teaspoon freshly ground black pepper

In a small saucepan over low heat, stir brown sugar, butter, and honey until melted and combined. Remove from heat and whisk in the oil, mustard, soy sauce, salt, and pepper. Cool for 5 minutes before using or storing. Keep for up to 30 days in a sealed container in the refrigerator.

When to Glaze

Typically the key ingredient to a glaze is sugar. It might be white sugar, brown sugar, or some other sweetener. Do not glaze your meat or seafood until just before you take it off the smoker; otherwise, you run the risk of burning it.

Simple Teriyaki Glaze

This easy-to-make classic teriyaki glaze tastes great on salmon, pork, and poultry.

INGREDIENTS | YIELDS 1 CUP (ENOUGH FOR 2 RACKS OF RIBS, 2 POUNDS OF SALMON, OR A WHOLE CHICKEN)

½ cup store-bought teriyaki glaze

¼ cup orange juice

2 tablespoons honey

1 tablespoon sesame oil

1 tablespoon rice vinegar

2 teaspoons minced ginger

1 teaspoon minced garlic

3 drops Sriracha hot sauce

Combine all ingredients in a small saucepan over low heat. Stir until all ingredients are melted and blended. Use immediately or refrigerate in a sealed container for up to 30 days.

Apricot-Habanero Glaze

Although this glaze will work with just about anything, it's ideal for salmon and shrimp. The habanero is a perfect complement to the apricot preserves and sultanas.

INGREDIENTS | YIELDS ½ CUP

½ teaspoon finely chopped dried habanero

½ teaspoon kosher or sea salt

1 tablespoon unsalted butter

2 tablespoons dark brown sugar

12 whole dried sultanas or golden raisins, chopped

3 tablespoons apricot preserves

1 teaspoon white wine vinegar

Combine all ingredients in a medium saucepan over low heat. Stir until all ingredients are melted and blended. Use immediately or refrigerate in a sealed container for up to 30 days.

Cranberry-Lemon Glaze

Cranberry and lemon are a fantastic and flavorful combination. Use this sweet glaze on poultry or pork for a year-round holiday flavor.

INGREDIENTS | YIELDS ¾ CUP (ENOUGH FOR 4 RACKS OF RIBS OR 2 WHOLE TURKEYS)

1 (8-ounce) can jellied cranberry sauce
½ teaspoon finely shredded lemon peel
2 tablespoons lemon juice
⅛ teaspoon crushed dried rosemary

Combine all ingredients in a medium saucepan over low heat. Stir until all ingredients are melted and blended. Use immediately or refrigerate in a sealed container for up to 30 days.

Red-Hot Apple Glaze

Cinnamon Red Hots candies make an excellent complement to a meat that has been seasoned with a spicy rub. And if any glaze is leftover, you can pour it over ice cream.

INGREDIENTS | YIELDS 2½ CUPS

2 cups apple juice
¼ cup Red Hots candies
2 tablespoons pectin
2 cups sugar

1. Place apple juice, Red Hots, and pectin in a medium saucepan over high heat. Bring to a full rolling boil, stirring constantly.

2. Add the sugar and bring mixture back to a boil. Boil, stirring constantly, for 5 minutes. Strain off any foam. Let cool slightly. Use immediately or store in an airtight container for up to 14 days.

The World's Easiest Glaze

It just doesn't get any easier than melting a jar of pepper jelly and using it to glaze anything you want to put on the smoker.

INGREDIENTS | YIELDS 9 OUNCES

1 (9-ounce) jar hot pepper jelly

Open jar and spoon jelly into a small saucepan. Heat jelly in the saucepan over low heat until melted. Use immediately or store in a sealed container in the refrigerator for up to 30 days.

CHAPTER 7

Beef and Lamb

Beef takes on smoke flavor very easily. Just about any wood you can smoke with will work with beef; some may be better than others, but you typically don't have to worry about the wood you have. Lamb is a leaner meat and needs to be cooked faster to keep it from drying out. Adding smoke flavor with herbs and spices is a good way to do this. If you are smoking, use hickory or oak wood to complement the natural flavor of the lamb.

RECIPES

Stovetop Smoked Beef Ribs

Smoking these ribs for two hours will get you a nice flavor without the risk of the smoke being overpowering. When selecting beef ribs, look for ribs with lots of meat between the bones. Don't be afraid of ribs with a heavy marbling of fat. That fat provides flavor and will keep the ribs from drying out. Serve these ribs with sauce on the side.

INGREDIENTS | SERVES 4

3 tablespoons kosher or sea salt

2 tablespoons freshly ground black pepper

2 tablespoons brown sugar

1 tablespoon paprika

½ teaspoon crushed red pepper flakes

2 (5–7 pound) racks beef ribs, membrane removed

How to Remove Rib Membranes

Set the rack of ribs on a cutting board with the meat side down. Insert a kitchen knife under a loose end of membrane. Work the knife under the membrane until you have enough loosened to grab. Grab membrane with a paper towel and pull.

1. Set up stovetop smoker according to the manufacturer's instructions. Make sure your kitchen is well vented to keep the smoke from filling the house.

2. In a small bowl, combine the salt, pepper, brown sugar, paprika, and red pepper flakes. Sprinkle the rub on both sides of the ribs and rub into the meat with your hands.

3. Cut the racks of ribs in half. Place ribs in smoker on a wire rack. Cover smoker with foil and turn heat to high. When smoke appears, lower heat to medium and smoke ribs for 2 hours.

4. Preheat oven to 200°F. Place ribs on a baking sheet and bake in the oven until tender (about 5 hours). Cut into individual ribs.

Stovetop Smoker Beef Jerky

Want to impress your friends with an easy-to-make jerky they can snack on during a football game? Give this recipe a try. Don't let the short ingredients list fool you—this jerky is packed with flavor. If you don't know how to cut the meat for jerky, just ask your butcher to cut it for you.

INGREDIENTS | SERVES 4

2 tablespoons kosher or sea salt

2 tablespoons brown sugar

1 pound bottom-round beef roast, thinly sliced

1. Set up stovetop smoker according to the manufacturer's instructions. Make sure your kitchen is well vented to keep the smoke from filling the house.

2. Place salt and brown sugar in a resealable a gallon-sized plastic bag and shake to mix. Add beef slices to the bag. Squeeze as much air as possible out of the bag and seal. Using your hands, squeeze the bag to cover the beef with the salt and sugar mixture. Refrigerate 6 hours.

3. Drain the beef in a colander, but do not rinse. Pat dry with paper towels. Lay the beef strips on the rack in the smoker. Place smoker over medium heat. Smoke for 2 hours.

4. Preheat oven to 200°F. Place the beef on a rack over a baking sheet. Cook until the beef is dry, but still a little pliable. Store jerky at room temperature in a resealable plastic bag for a week.

Texas-Style Smoked Brisket

A Texas-style brisket is a great addition to your cookout menu. When this meat is seasoned and allowed to cure, it is guaranteed to be a crowd pleaser. Save the leftovers for some great chili later on.

INGREDIENTS | SERVES 6

2 tablespoons plus ¾ cup brown sugar, divided

1 tablespoon plus 2 teaspoons kosher or sea salt, divided

1½ tablespoons chili powder

2 tablespoons freshly ground black pepper, divided

1 tablespoon cumin

1 tablespoon garlic powder

4 tablespoons paprika, divided

1 (4–5 pound) beef brisket, with fat cap on

4 cups ketchup

½ cup vinegar

⅓ cup yellow mustard

2 tablespoons hot pepper sauce

1 tablespoon garlic powder

1 teaspoon dried thyme

1. The night before you plan to cook the brisket, combine 2 tablespoons brown sugar, 1 tablespoon salt, chili powder, 1 tablespoon black pepper, cumin, garlic powder, and 2 tablespoons paprika in a small bowl. Place brisket on a baking sheet. Work all of the mixture into the meat with your hands, including the fat cap.

2. Wrap the brisket in two layers of plastic wrap as tightly as possible. Place wrapped brisket on a clean baking sheet and refrigerate for at least 8 hours or overnight.

3. Remove brisket from refrigerator and allow to come to room temperature (about 45 minutes). Set up grill for indirect heat or preheat a smoker to 250°F.

4. Unwrap brisket and set on a large aluminum pan. Place pan on grill or in smoker. If using a grill, add wood chips to the charcoal and cover the grill.

5. Smoke brisket for approximately 6 hours or until the meat is tender and can easily be shredded with your fingers. (If using a charcoal grill, add additional charcoal and wood chips as needed. Occasionally add mesquite wood chips as needed and stoke the fire.) Baste the brisket often with its drippings.

6. To make the barbecue sauce, combine ketchup, ¾ cup brown sugar, vinegar, mustard, hot pepper sauce, 2 tablespoons paprika, garlic powder, thyme, and remaining salt and pepper in a medium saucepan over medium heat. Bring mixture to a slow boil, stirring frequently. Reduce heat to low and simmer until sauce thickens (about 20 minutes). Set aside to cool.

7. When the brisket is done, remove from grill or smoker and let stand 15 minutes. Cut across the grain and serve with barbecue sauce for dipping. Reserve any leftover juices for use in other recipes.

Smoked Prime Rib Roast

Smoking really brings out the rich, savory flavor of this popular beef dish.

INGREDIENTS | SERVES 8

4 cloves garlic, minced

1 tablespoon kosher or sea salt

2 tablespoons coarsely ground black pepper

1 tablespoon dried rosemary

1 teaspoon dried thyme

6 pounds beef rib roast

½ cup olive oil plus ¼ cup for coating roast, divided

1½ cups dry red wine

1½ cups red wine vinegar

1. Prepare the rub by combining garlic, salt, pepper, rosemary, and thyme in a small bowl. Remove rib roast from packaging and pat dry with paper towels. Allow the rib roast to sit at room temperature for 45 minutes.

2. Brush a light coat of olive oil over the whole roast. Coat the entire roast with the rub. Work the rub into the meat with your hands.

3. Combine the red wine, vinegar, and ½ cup olive oil in a bowl. Whisk to mix completely. Set aside.

4. If using a gas or charcoal grill, create two or three smoke bombs (see instructions in Chapter 3). Add the smoke bombs to the grill every 20 minutes to keep the smoke going during the cooking time.

5. Set up grill for indirect cooking with charcoal or gas burners on both sides, and preheat to medium heat. Place an aluminum pan in the middle between the heat sources and fill two-thirds with water. Place rib roast in the middle of the grill grates directly over the water pan. Pour red wine mixture gently over the whole roast. The wine mixture should cover the roast, with the excess falling into the water pan. Cover the grill.

6. If using a smoker, preheat to 250°F. Place a water pan on the grates with a rack over the top. Place the rib roast on the rack and pour the wine mixture over the top.

7. Smoke the rib roast until the internal temperature reaches 145°F for medium rare, about 4 hours. Add more water if necessary to water pan. Remove roast from smoker. Allow to rest for 15 minutes. Slice and serve.

Smoked Korean-Style Beef Ribs

Korean short ribs are loaded with zesty flavor. They are tender but not mushy when cooked properly. Soy sauce and vinegar add a layer of Asian flair to these delicious ribs.

INGREDIENTS | SERVES 2

½ cup soy sauce

2 tablespoons rice vinegar

½ cup water

2 tablespoons brown sugar

1 tablespoon granulated sugar

2 cloves garlic, minced

1 ripe Bosc pear, peeled, cored, and coarsely chopped

1-inch piece fresh ginger, peeled and sliced

1 green onion, trimmed and coarsely chopped

2 teaspoons sesame oil

1 teaspoon kosher or sea salt

1½ pounds flanken-cut beef short ribs

An Apple Will Work Too

Traditional Korean short ribs are made with pears in the marinade. If you can't find a ripe pear, you can use a ripe red apple. The flavor will be slightly different, but still great.

1. To make the marinade, pulse the soy sauce, vinegar, water, brown sugar, granulated sugar, garlic, pear, ginger, green onion, sesame oil, and salt in a blender or food processor until combined.

2. Place the short ribs in a baking dish or resealable plastic bag and pour marinade over them. Cover dish with plastic wrap or seal plastic bag. Refrigerate at least 8 hours or overnight.

3. Preheat your smoker to high heat. Remove ribs from marinade. Place ribs on your smoker grates and smoke until done, about 3 hours. You'll know the ribs are done because the meat is so tender it's almost falling off the bone.

4. If you prefer some char on your ribs, heat your charcoal or gas grill to high. When the ribs come off the smoker, quickly grill the ribs on each side for 1 minute to caramelize the sugars in the marinade.

Smoked Beef Kebabs

There is just something appealing about eating meat on a stick. If you're using bamboo or wooden skewers, don't forget to soak them in water for about 30 minutes before skewering the beef.

INGREDIENTS | SERVES 6

3 cloves garlic, minced

2 teaspoons smoked paprika

½ teaspoon ground turmeric

1 teaspoon ground cumin

1 teaspoon kosher or sea salt

½ teaspoon freshly ground black pepper

⅓ cup red wine vinegar

½ cup olive oil

2 pounds boneless beef sirloin, cut into 1½-inch cubes

1. In a food processer or blender, combine garlic, paprika, turmeric, cumin, salt, pepper, and red wine vinegar. With the food processor or blender running slowly, pour in the olive oil. Blend until mixture is smooth.

2. Place beef cubes in a large bowl or resealable plastic bag. Pour the marinade over the meat and toss to coat. Cover bowl or seal plastic bag. Refrigerate at least 2 hours.

3. Set up grill for direct heat cooking and preheat to high. Make a smoke bomb (see instructions in Chapter 3) and set aside.

4. Remove meat from marinade, discard remaining marinade, and thread meat onto metal or presoaked bamboo skewers.

5. Place smoke bomb on the charcoal and close the lid. When smoke starts to appear, place the meat skewers on the grill and cook 2 minutes per side (for rare) or 3 minutes per side (for medium) with the lid closed. When done, remove from grill, tent with foil, and allow to rest for 3 minutes before serving.

Smoked Beef Enchilada Casserole

A smoked beef chuck roast is a versatile ingredient for a variety of different dishes. Don't be afraid to use this recipe using other meats, especially if you've got some leftover smoked brisket. For an added flavor, top the casserole with some smoked cheese.

INGREDIENTS | SERVES 8

1 (3-pound) beef chuck roast

1 package taco seasoning

2 tablespoons olive oil

1 large onion, peeled and diced

1 large green bell pepper, cored, seeded, and diced

2 jalapeño peppers, cored, seeded, and finely diced

1 (10-ounce) can diced tomatoes

1 (4-ounce) can diced green chiles

2 (10-ounce) cans red enchilada sauce

2 pounds shredded Mexican-blend cheese

18 corn tortillas

Cook It in Your Smoker

You can heat the foil-covered casserole dish on the grill or in the smoker for the same amount of time as in the oven. When the dish is uncovered during the last 15 minutes of cooking, the cheese and beef will have a smoke flavor.

1. Set up your grill or smoker for indirect heat cooking and preheat to medium heat. If using a gas or charcoal grill, create two or three smoke bombs (see instructions in Chapter 3) and set aside. Season all sides of the chuck roast with the taco seasoning.

2. Place one smoke bomb on the hot coals and then place the grill grate over the smoke bomb, the chuck roast on the grill grate, and cover. Replace smoke bombs and add charcoal as needed. Smoke until the internal temperature of the roast reaches 165°F, about 3 hours. Remove from grill and wrap tightly in a double layer of foil. Return to the grill and continue to cook until temperature reaches 200°F, about 2 hours. Remove from grill or smoker and allow to cool slightly, about 5–10 minutes, before shredding beef. (Beef can be refrigerated for up to 2 days before making casserole. Bring to room temperature before assembling.)

3. Heat olive oil in a medium skillet over medium heat. Lightly sauté the onions, bell peppers, and jalapeños until tender, but not browning (about 5 minutes). Set aside.

4. Combine tomatoes and chilies in a medium-size bowl. Add sautéed vegetables and enchilada sauce, and stir to mix.

5. Spray the bottom of a 9" × 13" casserole dish with nonstick cooking spray. Spoon a layer of enchilada-sauce mixture over the bottom of the casserole dish. Layer corn tortillas over the sauce, followed by a layer of cheese, a layer of beef, and a layer of sauce. Repeat three times until casserole dish is full. Top with a generous portion of cheese.

6. Preheat oven to 350°F. Cover casserole dish with foil and bake for 45 minutes. Remove foil and bake another 15 minutes until the cheese is melted and golden brown.

Thai Smoked Beef Salad

If you're having trouble getting your family to eat their greens, add a few slices of properly smoked beef to the next salad you serve. It might just do the trick!

INGREDIENTS | SERVES 6

6 tablespoons fresh lime juice

2½ tablespoons Thai fish sauce

1 fresh Thai or serrano chile, seeded and finely chopped

1 teaspoon sugar

2 teaspoons finely chopped fresh cilantro

2 teaspoons finely chopped fresh mint

4 green onions, thinly sliced on the diagonal

12 ounces baby arugula (about 5 cups)

3 shallots, thinly sliced into rings

3 Kirby cucumbers, peeled, halved lengthwise, and cut into ¼-inch-thick half-moons

2 tablespoons olive oil

1 (1½-pound) boneless sirloin steak

½ teaspoon kosher or sea salt

½ teaspoon freshly ground black pepper

½ cup unsalted peanuts, coarsely chopped (about 2½ ounces)

Kirby Cucumbers

The Kirby cucumber is the most popular cucumber for making pickles. But the Kirby is also popular in salads and as a side dish because of it's tender rind and mild flavor.

1. Set up your grill for indirect heat and preheat to medium-low.

2. Whisk together the lime juice, fish sauce, chile, and sugar in a small bowl until the sugar is dissolved. Stir in the cilantro and mint. Set dressing aside.

3. In a large bowl, combine the green onions, arugula, shallots, and cucumbers. Set aside.

4. Brush the olive oil over the steaks and season with salt and pepper. Place steak on the cool side of the grill. Add wood chips to the coals, cover, and cook until the internal temperature reaches 130°F, about 1 hour. Remove steak from grill and increase heat to high as quickly as possible. Sear steak for 2 minutes per side. Transfer to a serving platter and allow to rest 5 minutes before serving.

5. Slice steak across the grain into ¼-inch-thick slices. Add steak slices to the arugula mixture. Drizzle with dressing and toss. Top with peanuts. Serve.

Shredded Smoked Beef Sandwiches

Adding the smoke before braising the meat will give this dish an amazing flavor. Don't skimp on the bread—buy a good firm roll that will hold up to the juiciness of the meat.

INGREDIENTS | SERVES 6

1 (3-pound) beef rump roast

¼ cup Santa Maria Seasoning (see recipe in Chapter 5)

1 medium onion, peeled and sliced

4 garlic cloves, minced

2 jalapeño peppers, cored, seeded, and sliced

1 green bell pepper, cored, seeded, and sliced

1 bottle beer, at room temperature

¼ cup Worcestershire sauce

6 slices provolone cheese

6 sandwich rolls

1. If using a gas or charcoal grill, set the grill up for indirect heat cooking. Preheat grill or smoker to 225°F.

2. Season roast with Santa Maria Seasoning. Place seasoned roast on grill or smoker rack and cook for 3 hours or until the internal temperature reaches 150°F.

3. Place onions, garlic, and peppers in a medium foil pan. Add beer and Worchestershire sauce to vegetables and stir to mix. Place roast in the center of the pan on top of the onions and peppers. Cover tightly with foil and return to the grill. Increase temperature of the grill or smoker to 275°F and smoke until the roast is tender and the internal temperature is 200°F (about 3 hours).

4. Allow to rest 20 minutes before slicing and serving.

Leftover Smoked Brisket Chili

Even though this dish is usually made with leftover brisket, you'll often find yourself making brisket just to make chili. Serve the beans on the side if some of your guests prefer no-bean chili.

INGREDIENTS | SERVES 8

Beans:

1 cup dried pinto beans
1 large onion, peeled and chopped
2 cloves garlic, minced
1 teaspoon dried oregano

Chili:

3 tablespoons olive oil
2 large onions, peeled and chopped
4 cloves garlic, minced
3 tablespoons ancho chile powder
1 tablespoon dried oregano
1 tablespoon ground cumin
¼ teaspoon cayenne pepper
2 teaspoons kosher or sea salt, divided
1½ teaspoons freshly ground black
  pepper, divided
1 (28-ounce) can diced tomatoes
1 (12-ounce) bottle lager beer
1 (6-ounce) can tomato paste
4 cups diced leftover smoked brisket
1½ cups leftover brisket juice

Garnishes

Chili garnishes can be almost as much fun as the chili. Serve chili with warm corn tortillas, sour cream, sliced avocado, minced onion, cilantro leaves, or salsa. For something a little different, serve the chili over French fries, cooked pasta, or cooked rice.

1. Soak the pinto beans in a medium bowl covered by at least 2 inches of water overnight. The next morning drain the beans. In a medium saucepan, cover the beans with cold water and add onion, garlic, and oregano. Bring the beans to a boil over high heat. Reduce heat to low and simmer until tender, about 1 hour. Drain beans and set aside.

2. To make the chili, heat the oil in a heavy-bottomed 6-quart stockpot over medium heat. Add the onions and cook until tender and somewhat translucent, about 15 minutes. Add garlic, chili powder, oregano, cumin, cayenne, 1 teaspoon salt, and ½ teaspoon black pepper. Cook for 2 minutes. Add tomatoes with their juice, beer, and tomato paste. Stir to combine.

3. Add the leftover brisket and juices to the pot. Cover, increase heat to medium-high, and bring to a boil. Reduce heat to low and simmer about 30 minutes or until the meat is starting to fall apart. Season with remaining salt and pepper.

4. Serve the beans on the side or add them to the chili during the last 15 minutes of cooking.

Marinated and Smoked Leg of Lamb

Leg of lamb should never be overcooked. Cook lamb to medium-rare or medium to avoid drying it out.

INGREDIENTS | SERVES 8

1 (5–6 pound) leg of lamb
2 bunches green onions, coarsely chopped
1 small onion, peeled and chopped
8 garlic cloves, minced
½ cup chopped fresh cilantro
1 tablespoon chopped fresh thyme
2 tablespoons grated fresh ginger
2 tablespoons packed brown sugar
¼ cup paprika
2 tablespoons cumin
1 tablespoon ground coriander
⅛ cup olive oil

1. Place the lamb on a cutting board and use a sharp knife to make a few 6–8½-inch-long deep cuts over the surface of the leg of lamb. Place lamb in a large glass or plastic dish.

2. In a medium-size bowl, combine green onions, onion, garlic, cilantro, thyme, ginger, brown sugar, paprika, cumin, and coriander. Mash all the ingredients until they form a paste. Slowly add olive oil a little at a time, stirring until ingredients are combined.

3. Rub mixture over the leg of lamb, using your hands to work some of the marinade into the cuts you made. Cover pan with plastic wrap and refrigerate overnight.

4. If using a gas or charcoal grill, create two or three smoke bombs (see instructions in Chapter 3) and set aside.

5. Set up your grill for indirect heat cooking. Preheat grill or smoker to medium heat.

6. If using a grill, place a foil pan in the middle of the grill with the hot coals on either side. Fill pan with water. Add smoke bombs to charcoal. Place lamb on grill grate over water pan.

7. Cover grill and cook until internal temperature of lamb reaches 145°F (about 3 hours). Turn lamb every hour to make sure it cooks evenly. Add more water to pan when needed. Replace smoke bombs when they stop smoking.

Grilled and Smoked Lamb Chops

Rosemary smoke delicately perfumes these delectable lamb chops.

INGREDIENTS | SERVES 4

10 large sprigs rosemary

2 cloves garlic, crushed

1 teaspoon kosher or sea salt

2 tablespoons olive oil

2 tablespoons fresh lemon juice

8 bone-in loin lamb chops, about
   1¼-inch thick

Barbecue Rosemary

You can find regular rosemary sprigs in the produce department of any grocery store, but if you want to use extra-large, sturdy rosemary stems as barbecue skewers, look for a barbecue rosemary (*Rosmarinus officinalis*) plant at your local nursery. Barbecue rosemary can be used to create smoke as well as to skewer food, but the flavor is too strong to use as a replacement for traditional rosemary in recipes.

1. Set up your gas or charcoal grill for direct and indirect heat. Preheat the grill to 450°F.

2. Remove the leaves from 1 rosemary sprig and chop leaves finely. In a large bowl combine the chopped rosemary, garlic, salt, oil, and lemon, and whisk to mix completely. Add chops to the bowl and toss to coat. Soak the remaining rosemary sprigs in water.

3. Place the lamb chops on the direct heat side of the grill. Cook for 3 minutes per side. The meat should brown but not burn. Use tongs to move the chops to the indirect-heat side of the grill. Remove the rosemary sprigs from the water and toss them on the charcoal or over the heat on a gas grill. Cover grill and cook for 3–4 minutes longer. Add more rosemary if you want a strong rosemary smoke flavor.

Pulled Chicken Sliders (Chapter 10)

Sweet Potato Cornbread (Chapter 11)

Carolina Pulled Pork Sandwich Slaw (Chapter 11)

Teriyaki Chicken Skewers (Chapter 10)

Macaroni Salad (Chapter 11)

Texas Table Sauce (Chapter 6)

Smoked Tomato Sauce (Chapter 12)

Stovetop Smoker Beef Jerky (Chapter 7)

Smoked Shrimp Tacos with Cumin-Cilantro Sauce (Chapter 9)

Smoked Beef Enchilada Casserole (Chapter 7)

Smoked Lobster Macaroni and Cheese
(Chapter 9)

Pig Candy (Chapter 13)

Smoked Skirt Steak (Chapter 7)

The Naked Fatty (Chapter 8)

Plank-Smoked Corn on the Cob (Chapter 14)

Asian-Inspired Pork Burgers (Chapter 8)

Smoked Acorn Squash Soup (Chapter 12)

Brown-Sugar Salmon Glaze (Chapter 6)

Bacon-Wrapped Jalapeño Poppers (Chapter 8)

Smoked-Butter Crab Cakes (Chapter 9)

Cola Barbecue Sauce (Chapter 6)

Smoked Summer Vegetable Kebabs (Chapter 12)

Smoked Apple Pie (Chapter 13)

Smoked Chicken Salad (Chapter 10)

Stovetop Pecan-Smoked Leg of Lamb

This easy-to-make lamb dish is packed with flavor and can be made in your kitchen. Try it when it's too cold to cook outside.

INGREDIENTS | SERVES 8

6 garlic cloves

2 tablespoons chopped fresh parsley

¼ cup olive oil

¼ cup white wine

1 tablespoon dried rosemary

1 (5-pound) leg of lamb

1 tablespoon kosher or sea salt

2 tablespoons pecan wood chips

1 (6-ounce) jar jalapeño jelly

1. Chop garlic and parsley together to make a paste. Place paste in a small bowl and mix with olive oil, wine, and rosemary. Place leg of lamb in a large resealable plastic bag or in a 9" × 13" dish. Pour marinade over lamb. Cover and refrigerate for up to 6 hours.

2. Remove lamb from marinade, reserving the marinade. Set up stovetop smoker, according to the manufacturer's directions, using pecan wood chips. Pour half of the reserved marinade into the drip pan of the smoker, place the lamb on the rack, season with salt, and cover tightly with foil. Smoke for 1 hour over medium heat.

3. Remove foil and brush lamb with remaining marinade. Preheat oven to 350°F. Roast lamb until the interior temperature reaches 145°F (about 1 hour). Remove from oven and allow to rest for 10 minutes. Slice and serve with jalapeño jelly on the side.

Smoke-Grilled Lamb Ribs with Oregano, Lemon, and Honey

Use a little caution when cooking these little ribs, because they can go from tender and juicy to tough and dry pretty quickly.

INGREDIENTS | SERVES 4

3 tablespoons dried oregano

3 tablespoons garlic salt

2 tablespoons smoked paprika

2 tablespoons toasted and ground coriander seeds

1 tablespoon freshly ground black pepper

2 teaspoons kosher or sea salt, divided

6 racks lamb spareribs

Juice of 2 lemons

3 tablespoons honey

¼ cup red wine vinegar

2 garlic cloves, minced

1 cup minced red onion

3 lemons, cut in half

3 tablespoons extra-virgin olive oil

3 tablespoons fresh oregano leaves

1. In a small bowl, combine dried oregano, garlic salt, paprika, coriander, pepper, and 1 teaspoon salt. Brush ribs with lemon juice. Coat all sides of the ribs with the oregano mixture, making sure the seasoning is evenly spread over the ribs.

2. If using a gas or charcoal grill, create two or three smoke bombs (see instructions in Chapter 3) and set aside.

3. Set up your grill or smoker for indirect heat. Preheat smoker to low. Place ribs on the grill, making sure the ribs are not directly over the heat. Smoke for 1 hour using a smoke bomb directly on the coals.

4. Make the glaze: Combine honey, vinegar, garlic, remaining salt, and red onion in a small saucepan. Heat slightly over medium heat to soften honey and stir to combine.

5. Place two racks of ribs on a large piece of foil, overlapping the rib racks. Brush about a third of the glaze over the ribs. Fold foil over and seal tightly. Repeat two more times with remaining ribs and glaze.

6. Return foiled ribs to the grill, meat side down, and cook for 30 minutes. Carefully flip ribs over and grill for another 30 minutes. Remove ribs packets from the grill and allow to rest in the foil for 20 minutes.

7. While ribs are resting, grill the lemons over direct heat until grill marks form (about 5 minutes).

8. Remove ribs from foil and grill for 2 minutes per side on a hot grill. Remove ribs and drizzle with olive oil. Serve with grilled lemons and oregano leaves as a garnish.

Smoked Skirt Steak

Smoked skirt steak is versatile meat—you can chop it up for tacos or slice it for sandwiches or salads. Double the recipe and keep some in the freezer for a quick and easy dinner.

INGREDIENTS | SERVES 4

1 large onion, peeled and roughly chopped

1 jalapeño pepper, chopped

2 garlic cloves, chopped

Juice of 1 lemon

1 teaspoon kosher or sea salt

1 tablespoon freshly ground black pepper

1 pound skirt steak

1. Place the onion, jalapeño, garlic, lemon juice, salt, and pepper in a resealable plastic bag. Seal and shake to mix. Add the steak and seal again, squeezing as much air out of the bag as possible. Refrigerate for 1 hour, turning over every 15 minutes.

2. While skirt steak marinates, set up grill for indirect heat. Preheat to medium-high.

3. Remove steak from plastic bag and discard marinade. Place on cool side of the grill and smoke, using a strong wood like mesquite, oak, or hickory, until meat has reached an internal temperature of 130°F (about 20 minutes). Move meat to the hot side of the grill, directly over the coals. Sear each side for 2 minutes or until grill marks appear.

4. Place cooked steak on a cutting board and allow to rest for 5 minutes. Cut against the grain into thin slices and serve immediately.

CHAPTER 8

Pork

Depending on what cut of pork you are cooking, this meat can be one of the most forgiving to smoke, or one of the most unforgiving. Today's pork products are some of the leanest cuts of meat on the market. Because of the lack of fat in cuts like chops, loins, and tenderloins, they require more care when cooking than cuts like pork belly, butts, and shoulders. A little caution and cooking practice will get you flavorful dishes that taste great.

RECIPES

Buckboard Bacon

Buckboard bacon is close in flavor to Canadian bacon or ham, and is a great-tasting alternative in many breakfast dishes. Use it in omelets or hash, season beans with it, or fry thin slices for a unique and tasty sandwich meat.

INGREDIENTS | SERVES 4

1 pork loin (see sidebar)

1 tablespoon Morton Tender Quick curing salt

1 tablespoon dark brown sugar

1 teaspoon garlic powder

1 teaspoon onion powder

1 tablespoon Grade A maple syrup

Dry Cure Ingredient Ratios

The most important step in curing meat is to determine the necessary amount of dry cure mixture. Carefully weigh the pork loin and calculate precisely how much dry cure you need. The ingredients listed here are per pound of pork loin. So, if your pork loin is 2½ pounds, multiply each cure ingredient by 2.5.

1. Place pork loin on a cutting board. With a sharp knife, carefully trim as much fat off the loin as you can.

2. Combine Tender Quick, brown sugar, garlic powder, and onion powder in a small bowl. Rub the dry cure over the entire surface of the pork loin.

3. Place pork loin in a resealable plastic bag. Add maple syrup to the bag. Squeeze as much air out of the bag as possible and seal tightly. Place plastic bag containing the pork in a 9" × 13" casserole dish or platter and refrigerate for 7–10 days, turning the pork loin over every day. Plan on 2 days per inch of meat for the curing time. You may notice liquid forming inside the bag as the salt draws out moisture from the pork. Do not drain the liquid; some of it will be drawn back into the meat.

4. Remove the pork loin from the plastic bag and rinse thoroughly. Fill a sink or a clean food-safe bucket with cold water. Place loin in water and soak for 30 minutes to remove as much excess salt from the loin as possible.

Remove loin from water and slice off a small piece. Fry the slice in a small skillet over medium-high heat until cooked through, about 5 minutes per side. Cool slightly and taste the slice for saltiness. If the piece is too salty for your taste, change the water in the sink or bucket and soak for another 30 minutes. After soaking, slice off another piece of pork loin and repeat the frying and tasting process until the salt level is acceptable to you. Pat the pork loin dry and return, uncovered, to the refrigerator overnight.

5. The next day, smoke the pork loin at a low temperature (about 225°F) until the internal temperature reaches 145°F, about 2 hours. At this point, the pork loin has been properly cured and smoked and is ready to be eaten.

Smoked Pork Tenderloin with Bourbon-Rosemary Sauce

Bourbon and rosemary provide a huge depth of flavor to the tenderloin. Serve with a bold side dish that won't get lost in the flavors of the pork.

INGREDIENTS | SERVES 6

½ cup bourbon

½ cup soy sauce

½ cup light brown sugar

Juice of 1 lemon

3 large rosemary sprigs, bruised

2 (1-pound) pork tenderloins

1 tablespoon vegetable oil

1 teaspoon kosher or sea salt

1 teaspoon freshly ground black pepper

How to Bruise Rosemary

Roll the rosemary sprigs lightly between the palms of your hands or fingers. Don't mash the sprigs; all you want to do is soften the leaves a little to allow the essential oils to escape when cooked.

1. In a large bowl, combine the bourbon, soy sauce, brown sugar, and lemon juice. Whisk to mix. Stir in the rosemary sprigs. Add the pork tenderloins and turn to coat. Allow the tenderloins to stand for 1 hour, at room temperature, turning halfway through.

2. Set up a stovetop smoker according to manufacturer's instructions, using ½ cup of dry smoke wood chips. Make sure your kitchen is well ventilated. Place drip tray and rack in the smoker. Preheat oven to 375°F.

3. Remove pork from marinade, discard rosemary sprigs, and reserve ½ cup of the marinade. Set the covered smoker on top of the stove over high heat. When smoke begins to rise from the sides of the smoker, set the pork on the rack. Cover and smoke for 10 minutes over low heat.

4. Using an ovenproof skillet, heat the oil until hot. Season the pork with salt and pepper and place in the skillet. Brown all sides of the pork tenderloin. Place the skillet in the oven and roast the pork, about 90 minuters or until it is pale pink in the middle. Transfer pork to a carving board and allow to rest for 5 minutes. Slice and serve.

Bacon-Wrapped Jalapeño Poppers

These addictive appetizers will be the hit of your tailgating event or party. Make more than you think you're going to need. They always disappear quickly.

INGREDIENTS | SERVES 6

¼ cup dry rub

8 ounces cream cheese, softened

6 medium jalapeño peppers

12 mini smoked sausages

1 pound thinly sliced bacon, each slice cut in half

Taming Jalapeño Peppers

If you like the flavor of jalapeños but don't want the heat that comes along with them, you can remove most of the spiciness by soaking the peppers in lemon-lime soda. Cut the peppers in half and remove the seeds and veins. Put the peppers in a large glass bottle and cover with soda. Refrigerate overnight and you'll have heatless jalapeños.

1. Preheat smoker to 225°F or set your grill up for indirect heat.

2. Mix 1 tablespoon of the dry rub into the cream cheese in a small bowl.

3. Wearing rubber gloves, cut the jalapeños in half lengthwise. Remove the seeds and veins.

4. Using a butter knife, spread cream cheese mixture into each jalapeño half. Place 1 mini smoked sausage on each jalapeño. Wrap each jalapeño half with a half-slice of bacon and secure with a toothpick. Season tops of the poppers with the remainder of the rub.

5. Smoke the jalapeños in a smoker or on the grill using indirect heat until the bacon is crisp, about 90 minutes. Remove from grill or smoker and allow to rest for 5 minutes. Serve warm.

Tea-Smoked Pork Belly

If you don't like the flavor of tea smoke, try using a mild apple wood or an herbal tea.

INGREDIENTS | SERVES 8

2½ pounds boneless pork belly, skin on

¼ cup plus 3 tablespoons canola oil, divided

⅓ cup soy sauce

⅓ cup rice wine

2 tablespoons sesame oil

2 tablespoons plus 2 teaspoons granulated sugar, divided

2 teaspoons kosher or sea salt

½ teaspoon freshly ground black pepper

⅔ cup lapsang souchong black tea

⅓ cup uncooked rice

⅓ cup brown sugar

1. Place the pork belly, skin side up, on a cutting board. Using a sharp knife or a fork, pierce the skin in 8 to 10 places. Turn over and repeat on the other side. Place pork belly in a resealable plastic bag and set aside.

2. In a medium bowl, mix ¼ cup canola oil, soy sauce, rice wine, sesame oil, 2 tablespoons granulated sugar, salt, and pepper. Whisk to combine. Pour marinade into plastic bag with pork belly. Squeeze as much air as possible out of the bag and seal. Work with your hands to insure the pork belly is completely coated. Refrigerate overnight.

3. Preheat your gas or charcoal grill to medium-high heat, 275–300°F. Keep the grill lid closed. Set up a stovetop smoker according to manufacturer's directions. Line the bottom of the smoker with foil to make cleanup easier. Spread the tea, rice, and brown sugar in the smoker box on top of the foil. Set smoker box aside.

4. Heat 3 tablespoons of canola oil in a heavy fry pan over medium heat until it starts to shimmer, about 1 minute. Add 2 teaspoons of granulated sugar to the oil. Heat the sugar while swirling the pan, until it starts to turn a dark golden-brown color. It should take less than a minute to reach this color. Place the pork belly, skin side down, in the pan and cook for 3 minutes without moving the pork. Turn over and cook another 3 minutes without moving the pork.

5. Place the pork belly, skin side up, in the stovetop smoker box. Cover the smoker box with the lid or with tightly wrapped foil. Place the smoker box on the grill, cover grill, and cook for 3 hours. Remove smoker box from the grill and allow the pork belly to rest, in the covered smoker, for 15 minutes. Slice and serve.

Smoked Pork Butt

Smoking a pork butt is only slightly more time-consuming than cooking it in a Crock-Pot. And only smoke can give you that authentic barbecue taste.

INGREDIENTS | SERVES 8

1 (5-pound) pork butt
½ cup dry rub

1. Remove pork butt from packaging and rinse. Pat dry. Spread the dry rub over the pork butt and rub it into the meat.

2. Preheat smoker to 225–250°F or set up your grill for indirect heat and preheat. If using a gas or charcoal grill, make three smoke bombs (see instructions in Chapter 3) and place them on the hot grill.

3. Smoke pork butt until internal temperature reaches 165°F (about 4 hours). Remove pork from the grill or smoker and wrap in a double layer of foil. Return the pork butt to the grill or smoker and cook until the internal temperature reaches about 200°F or a thermometer probe can be easily inserted into the meat, about 2 hours. (If you prefer, this step can be done in the oven. Place the wrapped pork butt in a preheated 200°F oven and bake for 2 hours.)

4. Remove pork from smoker, grill, or oven. Cool slightly, then shred the pork with two forks.

Cured and Smoked Trotters, Shanks, and Jowls

These rarely used parts of the hog are also some of the most flavorful. Trotters are great for seasoning beans, while shanks and jowls are wonderful for sandwiches and terrines.

INGREDIENTS | SERVES 8

1 gallon water

⅔ cup kosher salt

2 tablespoons Morton Tender Quick curing salt

1 cup sugar

1 tablespoon freshly ground black pepper

3 pounds fresh pork trotters, shanks, or jowls

1. In a large soup pot, combine all the ingredients, except the meat. Heat over medium-low heat until the salt, Tender Quick, and sugar are dissolved, about 5 minutes. Remove pan from stove and cool to room temperature. Refrigerate until cold.

2. Place the meat and brine in a plastic resealable bag or small bucket. Refrigerate and cure for 3 days.

3. Remove pork from brine, rinse, and soak in cold water for 30 minutes to remove excess salt. Allow to dry uncovered in the open air for 3 hours.

4. Using a smoker or a grill set up for indirect cooking, smoke over hickory or oak wood until the internal temperature reaches reach 160°F, about 4 hours. Remove from heat and allow to cool. Slice or pull the meat off the bones if desired.

MOINK Balls with Raspberry Balsamic Chipotle Glaze

A little bit of MOO (beef meatball) along with a little bit of OINK (bacon) make one of the most popular barbecue appetizers in the world. This easy-to-make dish uses premade frozen meatballs to keep things simple.

INGREDIENTS | SERVES 8

1 cup raspberry preserves

¼ cup balsamic vinegar

½ teaspoon chopped chipotle pepper in adobo sauce

1 pound cold, thinly sliced smoked bacon, each slice cut in half

24 premade frozen beef meatballs, thawed

4 bamboo skewers, soaked in water for 30 minutes

1 cup barbecue sauce

1. Combine raspberry preserves, balsamic vinegar, and chipotle in a small saucepan over low heat. Bring to a simmer, stirring frequently, until the preserves melt, about 5 minutes. Whisk until everything is mixed. Cook until reduced and thickened, about 10 minutes more. Remove from heat and set aside.

2. Wrap one half-strip of bacon around a meatball and thread onto presoaked bamboo skewer. Repeat for all 24 meatballs.

3. Preheat smoker to 250°F. Place skewers on the smoker and cook until bacon is almost crisp (about 75 minutes).

4. Brush a thin coat of barbecue sauce on the MOINK balls, turn skewers over, and brush on sauce again. Let smoke for about 10 minutes to set the sauce. Brush with sauce again.

5. Remove from smoker and allow to rest for 10 minutes. Remove from skewers and serve with additional sauce on the side.

Smoked Pork Chops with Apple

The sweetness of the apples and maple syrup really complement these melt-in-your-mouth glazed pork chops.

INGREDIENTS | SERVES 6

6 (¾-inch-thick) pork loin chops

1 cup apple juice

⅓ cup maple syrup

2 tablespoons cider vinegar

2 medium red apples, peeled, cored, and cut into wedges

1. Set up stovetop smoker according to manufacturer's directions and smoke pork loin chops, using apple wood, over low heat for 30 minutes. The smoker should be just hot enough to smoke and not cook the chops, about 90°F.

2. In a large skillet over medium-high heat, mix the apple juice, syrup, and vinegar until boiling. Reduce heat to low and add the smoked pork chops. Cook pork chops until the internal temperature reaches 145°F. Remove from skillet and allow to rest on a serving platter.

3. Add apple wedges to skillet and cook over low heat until tender, about 30 minutes. Spoon apples over the top of the chops and serve.

Double-Smoked Ham with Peach Glaze

A grocery store ham is usually fully cooked and already smoked, and it tastes great just like that. But, if you spend some additional time smoking the ham, you'll have something truly delicious!

INGREDIENTS | SERVES 12

1 (15-ounce) can peach halves in heavy syrup, drained

2 tablespoons soy sauce

1 tablespoon sweet sorghum syrup

¼ cup ketchup

1 (6-pound) semi-boneless, fully cooked ham

What Is Sweet Sorghum?

Sweet sorghum is a plant with a high sugar content. It's been used to make syrup in the United States since the mid 1800s but isn't as popular as it once was. If you can't find sorghum in your area, you can substitute molasses.

1. If using a grill, set it up for indirect cooking and create a couple of smoke bombs (see instructions in Chapter 3) using hickory or oak wood. Preheat smoker or grill to 235°F.

2. Combine peaches, soy sauce, sorghum, and ketchup in a food processor and pulse until smooth. Put the glaze in a small bowl and set aside.

3. Lay the ham, cut side down, on a cutting board. With a very sharp knife, carefully score the skin of the ham into a a diamond pattern. Cut the pattern by scoring the skin in 1-inch-wide strips on a diagonal both directions. Place the ham, cut side down, on the smoker. Smoke for 2 hours.

4. Brush a thick coating of glaze over the ham. Cook for another 30 minutes and brush with another coating of glaze. Cook for an additional 30 minutes and remove from grill. Place ham on a platter and brush on additional coat of glaze. Tent ham with foil and allow to rest for 15 minutes before slicing.

Easy Smoked Pork Spare Ribs

Cooking ribs this way is known as the 3–2–1 method. Once you're done smoking the meat, you'll have tender, yet not falling-off-the-bone and mushy, ribs. After the first three hours, you can finish them, if necessary, in the oven.

INGREDIENTS | SERVES 4

2 racks St. Louis–cut pork spare ribs

1½ cups dry rub

½ cup apple juice

St. Louis–Style Ribs

St. Louis–style ribs are racks of pork ribs that have the top part of the rib rack removed. You can buy St. Louis–cut ribs in most grocery stores, but if they don't have them, ask the butcher or meat cutter to cut a regular rack of ribs down for you. Make sure you take ribs tips home too, because you can cook those right along with your St. Louis–cut ribs.

1. Remove the membrane from the back of the ribs by inserting a butter knife under an edge of the ribs and working it until the membrane becomes loose. Using your hand and a paper towel, pull the membrane off. Rinse ribs and pat dry with a paper towel. Season with dry rub, using the full amount of rub.

2. Preheat your smoker or set up your grill for indirect heat to 225°F–235°F. If using a gas or charcoal grill, make two or three smoke bombs (see instructions in Chapter 3).

3. Place ribs on the smoker or grill, cover, and smoke for 3 hours. Try not to uncover ribs during this time.

4. After 3 hours, remove ribs from grill or smoker, and wrap each rack of ribs in a double layer of foil. Just before sealing the foil, pour ¼ cup apple juice over each rack. Seal and return to the grill, meat side down. Close lid and cook for 2 hours.

5. Remove ribs from the cooker. Pull ribs gently out of the foil and return to the cooker. Cook for 1 hour. (If you plan to sauce the ribs, put one light coat of sauce on the ribs after 20 minutes, followed by another thin coat 20 minutes later.) Remove from grill and allow to rest for 10 minutes before slicing and serving.

Smoked Pork Kebabs

Smoked paprika enhances these Spanish-inspired pork kebabs. The smoke, combined with the caramelization from the last step of grilling, increases the flavor even more. This is a great summertime meal.

INGREDIENTS | SERVES 8

⅓ cup finely chopped, fresh Italian parsley leaves and tender stems

¼ cup extra-virgin olive oil

2 tablespoons minced red onion

1 tablespoon sherry vinegar

1 tablespoon smoked paprika

2 teaspoons ground cumin

2 teaspoons minced garlic

¼ teaspoon ground cayenne pepper

½ teaspoon kosher or sea salt

2 (1-pound) pork tenderloins

2 large bell peppers, 1 red and 1 green, cored, seeded, and cut into 1¼-inch squares

1. In a small bowl, whisk the parsley, olive oil, onion, vinegar, paprika, cumin, garlic, cayenne, and salt until blended.

2. Remove the silver skin and excess fat from the tenderloins and cut in 1¼-inch cubes. Add pork and marinade to a resealable plastic bag. Squeeze out as much air as possible and seal bag tightly. Shake the bag a little to make sure the meat is covered. Refrigerate 4–6 hours.

3. If using bamboo skewers, soak the skewers in water for at least 30 minutes. Set your grill up for direct and indirect heat.

4. Remove pork from marinade. Thread pork onto skewers, alternating between pork and bell peppers. Place kebabs on the indirect heat side of the grill. Add wood chips or a smoke bomb to the direct heat side (see instructions for smoke bombs in Chapter 3). Smoke for 30 minutes.

5. Move the kebabs to the direct heat side of the grill. Grill for 6–8 minutes over the hot grill, turning once or twice. Remove from grill and allow to rest 5 minutes before serving.

The Naked Fatty

The Fatty was invented by Steve Hamous and has taken on a life of its own in the barbecue world. There are a variety of versions of the Fatty, but this recipe is the original one. It's the easiest and most versitile. Try it on biscuits for a quick morning breakfast or crumble it up for sausage gravy.

INGREDIENTS | SERVES 3

1 (1-pound) chub pork breakfast sausage

⅓ cup dry rub

Fatty Variations

One of the more popular ways of making a fatty is to stuff it. Roll the sausage out into about a ½-inch slab. Cover the sausage with your favorite ingredients like cheese, bacon, or vegetables. Roll the sausage up, carefully pinching the ends together to seal. Smoke the stuffed fatty just like the Naked Fatty.

1. Preheat smoker to about 250°F.

2. Remove chub of sausage from refrigerator and remove packaging. Rub entire surface of sausage with dry rub.

3. Smoke sausage chub with any wood smoke you have until it reaches an internal temperature of 165°F, about 90 minutes. Remove from smoker and allow to rest for 10 minutes before slicing.

Smoked Chili Verde

Pork chili verde can be served with sour cream, avocados, salsa, and lime wedges on the side. Or you can try it over white or brown rice, in a burrito or taco, or spooned over French fries. It doesn't really matter how you serve it, it's going to taste good! Make this chili a day or two beforehand—it will taste even better.

INGREDIENTS | SERVES 8

1 tablespoon kosher or sea salt

2 teaspoons chipotle chile powder

4 teaspoons dried oregano, divided

1 teaspoon garlic powder

1 teaspoon ground cumin

1 (4–5 pound) boneless pork shoulder (butt)

8 medium tomatillos, husked and rinsed

1 small (4-ounce) can chopped green chiles with liquid

4 garlic cloves, peeled

1 small onion, peeled and roughly chopped

¾ cup beer

¼ cup finely chopped fresh cilantro leaves

1 teaspoon hot pepper sauce

Quick and Easy Green Pork

If you're in a hurry, try using canned green enchilada sauce or chili verde sauce instead of making your own. The results will be good and it will be a whole lot less work for you.

1. In a small bowl, combine the salt, chile powder, 2 teaspoons oregano, garlic powder, and cumin. Cover the entire pork butt with the rub mixture. Using your hands, work the rub into the pork. Place the pork on a plate or cutting board and loosely cover. Let rest for 30 minutes at room temperature.

2. Purée the tomatillos, chiles, garlic, onion, 2 teaspoons oregano, and beer in a food processer or blender until smooth. Set aside at room temperature while pork cooks

3. Set up your grill or smoker for indirect heat cooking, with hot coals stacked on both sides of the grill, and preheat to medium, about 250°F. Place a disposable foil pan between the heat sources and fill ¾ of the way with water. Use a smoke bomb placed directly on the coals. When smoke starts to appear, place the pork butt on the grill grates directly over the drip pan of water. Close the lid and smoke the pork over medium heat for 30–45 minutes.

4. After smoking the pork butt, working as quickly as possible to help maintain grill temperature, place the pork in a large foil pan. Pour the tomatillo mixture around the pork, but not over the top of it. The pan

should be large enough that the tomatillo mixture only reaches about one inch up the pork. Cover the pan tightly with foil and return to the center of the cooking surface. Close the lid and continue to cook until the pork is fork tender and the internal temperature is 190°F (about 2½ hours). Remove the pork from the grill and immediately close the lid to maintain the temperature.

5. Place the pork on a cutting board and roughly chop and shred the pork into ½- to ¾-inch chunks. Remove any large pieces of fat that have not rendered out.

6. Carefully pour the cooking liquid into a large saucepan. With a large spoon, try to remove as much fat as you can from the surface. Add the cut-up pork. Cook for 10–15 minutes over low heat. Season with cilantro and hot sauce.

Smoky Cuban Sandwiches

Smoked pork loin is great in this famous Cuban sandwich. But you can also chop the pork for a tasty addition to a salad or slice it thinly and serve on crackers with a little cheese.

INGREDIENTS | SERVES 6

¼ cup fresh orange juice

¼ cup fresh lime juice

1 (3-pound) boneless pork loin roast

5 cloves garlic, minced

1 teaspoon cumin

1 teaspoon dried oregano

1½ teaspoon kosher or sea salt

½ teaspoon freshly ground black pepper

8 French rolls, split

2 tablespoons yellow mustard

8 thin slices deli ham

1 cup dill pickle chips

8 slices provolone cheese

Citrus Juices and Pork

Don't let the juice-injected pork sit too long. The acids in the juices will turn the pork to mush if allowed to rest for too long a period of time.

1. Mix orange and lime juice together and strain to remove pulp. Using a meat injector, inject the pork with juice mixture in several places. Try to inject evenly throughout the pork loin roast.

2. Combine the garlic, cumin, oregano, salt, and pepper in a small bowl. Coat the pork loin with the spice mixture and work into the meat with your hands. Wrap the pork loin as tightly as possible in a double layer of plastic wrap. Place the wrapped pork in a resealable plastic bag and refrigerate for 24 hours.

3. Set up your grill for indirect heat cooking, with coals stacked on both sides of the grill, preheat to medium, about 250°F. Place a disposable foil pan between the heat sources and fill ¾ of the way with water. Use your preferred method for generating smoke. When smoke starts to appear, place the pork butt on the grill grates directly over the drip pan of water. Close the lid and smoke the pork over medium heat for 1 hour.

4. Move pork loin to a hot section of the grill. Sear on all sides until browned (about 10 minutes), rotating the pork loin ¼ turn every 2 minutes. After searing, check the temperature using a thermometer inserted into the thickest section of the loin. If the temperature is below 140°F, return to indirect cooking until it reaches 140°F.

5. Remove the pork to a cutting board and allow to rest for 10 minutes. If using a charcoal grill, while pork is resting, spread coals out on the grill evenly. If using a gas grill, increase heat to high.

6. Spread mustard on one side of each roll. Place a slice of ham on each roll followed by a layer of dill pickle. Thinly slice pork and layer on top of pickles. Top the pork with a slice of provolone cheese. Place the top of the roll over the cheese.

7. Put the sandwiches on the grill over direct heat. Press down with a spatula for 2–3 minutes until cheese melts. Serve immediately.

Asian-Inspired Pork Burgers

Tired of the same old beef burgers? Try this twist on the old barbecue standby. And if you really want something different, use the pork mixture to make a smoked meat loaf.

INGREDIENTS | SERVES 4

1 pound ground pork
1 clove garlic, crushed
1 tablespoon grated fresh gingerroot
2 tablespoons soy sauce
1½ teaspoons garlic chili paste
4 hamburger rolls, toasted

1. Combine all ingredients in a bowl and gently mix together. Using your hands, form the mixture into 4 patties. Place patties on a plate and refrigerate while the grill preheats.

2. Set up grill for indirect cooking. Preheat to medium-high. Use a smoke bomb (see instructions in Chapter 3) or smoker box to generate heat with cherry wood.

3. Smoke patties on cool side of grill for 8 minutes.

4. On the stove in the kitchen or outside on the grill, heat a cast-iron skillet to very hot. As soon as the patties are smoked, quickly sear each side of the burger patties until they form a nice crust, about 2 minutes a side. Remove from skillet and allow to rest for 2 minutes. Serve on toasted rolls.

CHAPTER 9

Seafood

Seafood is one of the tastiest proteins for smoking. Not only do the natural oils in the fish work well with the smoke flavor, but they make the food a little healthier than meats. One of the most popular smoked dishes around is smoked salmon, but don't just stop there. Fish and seafood are versatile and can be eaten as a main dish or as an ingredient in other dishes, so try smoking as many different types of seafood and fish as possible to see which one you like the most.

RECIPES

Smoked Salmon

Smoked salmon is likely the most popular smoked seafood, but don't limit yourself to whole fillets. You can use the smoked salmon sliced and served with bread or make a salmon pâté.

INGREDIENTS | SERVES 4

1 teaspoon sugar

1½ teaspoon kosher or sea salt

¼ teaspoon freshly ground white pepper

1 (12–14 ounce) salmon fillet, skin on

1. In a small bowl combine the sugar, salt, and pepper. Place the salmon on a plate or cutting board, skin side down. Using fish tweezers, remove all the pin bones from the salmon. Rub the sugar mixture evenly over the top of the fillet.

2. Find a cast-iron skillet or heavy-bottomed stainless steel pan for smoking the salmon. Tear a piece of 18-inch-wide heavy-duty foil so it is three times as long as the skillet or pan is wide. Place the center of the foil strip in the middle of the skillet or pan. Press the foil carefully down into the skillet or pan so it forms around the inside. Add wood chips or wood dust to the skillet and place a small round rack in the skillet on top of the foil and wood.

3. Place the salmon fillet on top of the rack and bring the foil up over the top of everything, forming a tent. Leave a small opening at the top.

4. In a well-ventilated area, place the pan over medium-high heat until smoke starts to appear from the top of the foil tent. Reduce the heat to medium-low and crimp the foil closed at the top. Don't crimp too much; you want a dome formed so the smoke can circulate around the salmon. Cook the salmon for 10 minutes or until done. Open the foil to check for doneness; the salmon should be firm and opaque.

5. Remove salmon and serve as it is or chill and save for use in other recipes.

Super-Easy Smoked Salmon Chowder

This unique chowder will warm those chilly fall and winter evenings. Serve it with some fresh crusty bread and a green salad for a complete meal.

INGREDIENTS | SERVES 6

4 (10¼ -ounce) cans condensed cream of potato soup

4 soup cans whole milk, or more as needed

1 (8-ounce) package cream cheese, cut into small pieces

3 green onions, white and green parts thinly sliced crosswise

2 teaspoons hot pepper sauce

2 ears sweet corn, cooked and kernels removed

10 ounces Smoked Salmon, flaked (see recipe in this chapter)

3 strips bacon, cooked until crispy and then crumbled

Make It Creamier

For a richer and creamier texture in this chowder, try using half-and-half or cream instead of whole milk.

1. Combine soup, milk, cream cheese, green onions, and hot pepper sauce in a large saucepan over medium heat, stirring frequently until the soup is hot and creamy, about 12 minutes.

2. Stir in corn and cook for 4 minutes. Gently fold in the smoked salmon. Ladle the soup into bowls and top with bacon crumbles just before serving.

Smoked Salmon Pasta Salad

Smoked salmon elevates ordinary pasta salad and makes it a meal instead of side dish. The heavy cream adds a richness and creaminess that complements the smoked salmon perfectly.

INGREDIENTS | SERVES 4

¼ cup extra-virgin olive oil

1 shallot, chopped

1 cup heavy cream

3 tablespoons capers, drained

1 pound pasta, cooked al dente and drained

¼ cup reserved pasta cooking water

¼ pound Smoked Salmon, chopped (see recipe in this chapter)

1 teaspoon kosher or sea salt

1 teaspoon freshly ground black pepper

1. Heat olive oil in a large skillet over medium heat. Add shallot and cook, stirring frequently until tender but not browned (about 10 minutes). Add cream and capers.

2. Add pasta and toss to coat. Add reserved pasta cooking water a little at a time to thin the sauce.

3. Fold in smoked salmon and heat through. Season with salt and pepper and serve immediately.

Smoked Bacon-Wrapped Scallops

Bacon-wrapped scallops are a favorite just about everywhere. The bacon will help keep the scallops from drying out. Depending on the exact temperature of the grill or smoker, you may have to adjust the cooking time a little. Use the bacon as a judge for doneness. When the bacon is crisp, the scallops will be done.

INGREDIENTS | SERVES 4

8 large sea scallops

8 slices bacon

¼ cup melted butter

1 teaspoon kosher or sea salt

1 teaspoon freshly ground black pepper

1. Set up your grill for indirect heat cooking and preheat to medium heat. If using a smoker, preheat to 225°F.

2. Create a smoke bomb (see instructions in Chapter 3) to add to grill just before you add the scallops.

3. To prepare the scallops, wrap each scallop in one slice of bacon, securing the bacon in place with a toothpick. Brush scallops with melted butter and season with salt and pepper. Place scallops on a baking sheet and set the sheet on the grill over the unheated side of the grill.

4. Cook until scallops are done and bacon is crisp, about 15 minutes. Rotate the baking tray a couple of times during the cooking to ensure even cooking of the bacon. Remove from heat and serve immediately.

Smoked-Butter Crab Cakes

You don't have to smoke all the ingredients in this dish to get a smoky flavor. In this recipe, smoked butter adds the smoke flavor to a traditional crab cake.

INGREDIENTS | SERVES 4

¼ cup unsalted butter, frozen

½ cup finely chopped shallots

1 teaspoon sugar

2½ teaspoons garlic Season-All

1 teaspoon kosher or sea salt

½ teaspoon freshly ground black pepper

1 pound shredded claw crabmeat

1 pound lump crabmeat, picked through and any bits of shell removed

1½ cups panko bread crumbs

¾ cup mayonnaise

2 large eggs, lightly beaten

2 teaspoons fresh lemon juice

1. Melt the butter in skillet on the grill or in the smoker with a mild fruitwood smoke. Remove from heat and pour into a small bowl.

2. Increase heat of the grill to medium-high. Return 1 tablespoon of the smoked melted butter to the skillet. Add the shallots and sugar and cook until shallots are tender but not brown, about 10 minutes. Remove shallots from skillet and allow to cool.

3. In a medium bowl, whisk together garlic Season-All, salt, pepper, 2 tablespoons smoked butter, and the shallots. Gently fold in the crabmeat and panko bread crumbs, mayonnaise, eggs, and lemon juice. Use care to mix so you don't break up the lumps of crab meat. Divide the crabmeat mixture into 12 equal portions.

4. Line a baking sheet with wax paper and sprinkle a light layer of panko bread crumbs over the wax paper to help keep the crab cakes from sticking. Form each portion of crab mixture into patties about ¾-inch thick. Lay each crab cake on the wax paper as you make them. Cover completed crab cakes with another sheet of wax paper and refrigerate for 1 hour.

5. Return skillet to the grill and heat the remaining smoked butter over medium-high heat. Fry the crab cakes in the hot butter, about 3 minutes per side, until they brown. Remove from heat and serve immediately.

Indoor Smoked Shrimp

This recipe can be served on a salad or eaten with the dipping sauce. Shrimp is one of the easiest seafoods to smoke when done correctly, because it cooks really fast. By using a stovetop smoker, you can control the heat so you have less chance of overcooking.

INGREDIENTS | SERVES 4

1 cup apple cider or apple juice

¼ cup ketchup

½ cup apple cider vinegar

2 tablespoons Dijon mustard

3 tablespoons brown sugar

2 teaspoons Worcestershire sauce

1 teaspoon smoked paprika

½ teaspoon dry mustard

¼ cup olive oil

¼ cup roughly chopped fresh flat-leaf parsley

¼ cup dry sherry

2 teaspoons lemon zest

½ teaspoon hot pepper sauce

4 cloves garlic, minced

2 tablespoons minced shallot

2 pounds medium shrimp, tail on, peeled and deveined

1. Set up stovetop smoker according to manufacturer's instructions.

2. Simmer the apple cider in a medium saucepan over medium-high heat until reduced by half, about 10 minutes. Add the ketchup, apple cider vinegar, mustard, sugar, Worcestershire, paprika, and dry mustard. Bring to a simmer and cook until thickened (about 30 minutes). Set sauce aside.

3. Combine the oil, parsley, sherry, zest, hot sauce, garlic, and shallots in a resealable plastic bag. Add the shrimp to the bag, squeeze as much air out of the bag as possible, and seal. Gently work with hands to coat the shrimp. Refrigerate at least 30 minutes, but not longer than an hour.

4. In a stovetop smoker, add 2 tablespoons of hickory wood dust. Remove shrimp from marinade and place in smoker on a rack. Close smoker lid and turn heat to medium. Smoke the shrimp until done (about 10 minutes). The shrimp will be fully cooked when they are pink in color. Remove shrimp to a platter and serve with sauce for dipping.

Hot-Smoked Sablefish

Brining the sablefish with juniper berries and cayenne pepper, in addition to the lemon and brown sugar, will highlight the great flavor sablefish already has. Use the bottom of heavy pot or cast-iron skillet to crush the juniper berries.

INGREDIENTS | SERVES 4

1 quart boiling water

¾ cup kosher salt

¼ cup packed brown sugar

¾ teaspoon freshly ground black pepper

¼ teaspoon cayenne pepper

18 whole juniper berries, crushed

Zest of 1 lemon

1 bay leaf

1 (1-pound) sablefish fillet

2 tablespoons olive oil

1. In a large bowl, combine water, salt, brown sugar, black pepper, cayenne, juniper berries, lemon zest, and bay leaf. Stir to dissolve the salt and sugar. Gently heat in a small pot over low heat to help dissolve the solids. Cool to room temperature. Pour brine into a 9" × 13" baking dish, add sablefish, and cover with a plate to submerge the fish. Cover and refrigerate 4 hours.

2. Preheat grill and set up for indirect heat. Use either a smoke bomb (see instructions in Chapter 3) or a smoker box for wood chips.

3. Remove sablefish from the brine. Rinse fish and pat dry. Brush the skin side of the fish with oil. Place fish, skin side down, on the grill, away from the heat source. Cover and smoke until the sablefish is firm and opaque (about 15–20 minutes). Cooking time will depend on the thickness of the fillet. Remove from grill, cool slightly, and flake fish into bite-size pieces.

Smoked Sablefish Crostini

Sablefish, or Alaskan black cod, is a fantastic and easy fish to smoke. Its mild flavor and firm texture takes the heat well, and its oils work with vegetables or a rich pilaf. It's the combination of tomatoes and rye bread that make this all come together for a delicious appetizer.

INGREDIENTS | SERVES 6

1 cup halved or quartered cherry tomatoes

7 tablespoons olive oil, divided

2 teaspoons fresh lemon juice

1 teaspoon kosher or sea salt, divided

1 teaspoon freshly ground black pepper, divided

4 large green or purple basil leaves, thinly sliced, plus small leaves for garnish

1 bunch green onions, roots trimmed off

8 (¼-inch-thick) slices country-style rye bread

8 ounces cream cheese

8 ounces Hot-Smoked Sablefish (see recipe in this chapter)

½ cup thinly sliced Kirby or Persian cucumbers

1. Set up a grill for direct heat cooking and preheat to medium-hot.

2. Combine tomatoes, 1 tablespoon oil, lemon juice, ½ teaspoon salt, ½ teaspoon pepper, and sliced basil in a medium bowl. Toss and let stand at room temperature for 30 minutes.

3. Place green onions on a baking sheet and drizzle with 2 tablespoons of oil. Toss to coat and season with remaining salt and pepper. Using a grill pan or cast-iron skillet, grill the onions over high heat until tender, about 5 minutes, turning often. Remove onions and allow to cool slightly. Chop and add to tomato mixture.

4. Brush bread slices with remaining oil and grill until toasted, about 1 minute per side. Remove from grill and cut each slice diagonally.

5. Spread 1 tablespoon of cream cheese on each toast half. Top with smoked fish and tomato mixture. Garnish with small basil leaves and cucumber slices. Serve immediately.

Smoked Tuna Dip

Smoked tuna dip on a cracker or crostini makes a fantastic appetizer. Don't worry about buying the best tuna you can find—save yourself a little money by purchasing frozen tuna.

INGREDIENTS | SERVES 4

½ pound albacore tuna fillet

2 (8-ounce) packages Neufchâtel cheese, softened slightly

2 teaspoons Worcestershire sauce

1 teaspoon garlic powder

1 teaspoon kosher or sea salt

½ teaspoon hot pepper sauce

Smoked Chicken Dip

If you have some leftover smoked chicken, grind it up in the food processor and use it in this recipe instead of tuna.

1. Line the inside and lid of a wok with foil. Place 1 cup of alder wood chips in the bottom of the wok. Insert a small round cake rack over the top of the chips. Turn heat on high. When smoke begins to appear, place the tuna on the cake rack and cover the wok. Reduce heat to low. Tuna is considered done at medium-rare, when the internal temperature is 125°F. Smoke tuna for 30 minutes and check for doneness. If tuna isn't done after 30 minutes, keep smoking and check every 5 minutes until done. Remove from smoker and cool to room temperature.

2. Place tuna in a food processor. Add remaining ingredients and blend together until smooth. Spoon dip into a bowl, cover, and refrigerate until ready to serve.

Smoked Clams

Using a smoker to open your clams is a great way to add the smoke flavor while accentuating the brininess of the clams. Add these little morsels to your favorite pasta sauce or use them in clam chowder. Discard any clams that don't open on their own.

INGREDIENTS | SERVES 6

36 fresh clams

5 tablespoons unsalted butter, melted

6 cloves garlic

12 ounces beer, room temperature

Soaking Clams

It is important to soak your fresh clams prior to cooking. Clams live buried in the sand, and a lot of that sand can end up inside the clam. Soaking in cold water helps to remove the sand and other debris.

1. Place the clams in a large bucket or bowl. Fill bowl with cold water and allow clams to soak for no less than 2 hours before smoking. After soaking, go through the clams and discard any that have broken shells or are not sealed tightly. Wash the clams with a brush under running cold water.

2. Set up your smoker or grill for indirect heat. Preheat grill for low heat, about 200°F. Create a smoke bomb (see instructions in Chapter 3) or use a smoker box for wood chips.

3. Place clams in a disposable foil pan. In a medium bowl, whisk together the butter, garlic, and beer. Pour butter mixture over the top of the clams.

4. Put foil pan in smoker and add smoke bomb or smoker box. Close the lid or cover the grill and smoke the clams until they open (about 20 minutes). Keep the temperature of the grill as close to 200°F as possible during smoking. Add additional wood chips if needed.

Smoked Salmon Candy

Smoke, salmon, sugar, maple syrup! With ingredients like that, how can you possibly go wrong? This is a great appetizer or snack when you want something a little different. It's also a good way to get kids to try salmon if they are a little hesitant.

INGREDIENTS | SERVES 8

½ gallon water

1 cup pickling salt

2 pounds dark brown sugar

1 cup Grade A maple syrup

3 pounds salmon fillets, cut into ½-inch wide strips

¾ cup honey mixed with ¼ cup water

1. Bring the water to a boil in a large pan over high heat. Add the salt and brown sugar. Reduce heat to medium and stir until all the solids are dissolved, about 8 minutes. Remove from heat and stir in maple syrup. Allow brine to cool to at least room temperature before using.

2. Place salmon strips in a large bowl or in a plastic resealable bag. Cover the salmon with the brine and refrigerate for 24 hours.

3. Remove salmon from brine and rinse in cold water. Pat salmon dry and place on a rack. Allow to air-dry for 30 minutes at room temperature.

4. Set up smoker for indirect heat. Preheat smoker to between 180°F and 200°F. Make a smoke bomb (see instructions in Chapter 3) or use a smoker box for generating smoke.

5. Place salmon on a rack and place the rack in the smoker. Add wood chips and smoke until salmon has dried but is still moist. Mix honey and water together in a small bowl, whisking until blended. Baste salmon with honey-and-water mixture every 45 minutes. Remove from smoker and allow to cool before storing in the refrigerator in a covered container.

Smoked Lobster Macaroni and Cheese

Smoking the lobster before adding it to the mac and cheese will give this dish a deeper flavor that will hold up to the sharpness of the cheese. If you don't want to use smoked lobster, try smoking the cheese first.

INGREDIENTS | SERVES 10

Lobster tails to equal 2 pounds of meat (about 5–8 Maine lobster tails)

1 quart whole milk

1 stick unsalted butter, divided

½ cup all-purpose flour

1 tablespoon kosher or sea salt

½ teaspoon freshly ground black pepper

½ teaspoon nutmeg

4 cups grated Gruyère cheese

2 cups grated sharp white Cheddar cheese

4 cups cooked and drained elbow macaroni

1½ cups bread crumbs

How to Tell When Lobster Is Cooked

The lobster's shell will turn red when cooked, but this isn't the best way to tell if it is done. Check the tail meat—when it turns white, the lobster is cooked through.

1. Set up stovetop smoker according to manufacturer's directions. Place apple wood dust in the bottom of the smoker. Place lobster tails on the rack. Place the smoker on the stovetop and heat over medium heat until the wood dust starts to smoke. Close the smoker lid.

2. Smoke lobster tails for 15 minutes or until done. Allow lobster tails to cool, remove from the shell, and chop lobster meat into chunks. Set aside.

3. Preheat oven to 375°F.

4. In a medium saucepan, warm milk over medium heat. In a large pot, melt 6 tablespoons of butter over low heat. Add flour to butter and whisk for 2 minutes. Slowly add warm milk, whisking constantly. Cook for 2 minutes until thickened slightly and smooth.

5. Remove from heat and add salt, pepper, and nutmeg. Stir to mix. Add cheeses and mix well. Stir in macaroni and lobster. Pour mixture into a greased 9" × 13" baking dish.

6. In a small bowl, mix bread crumbs with remaining butter. Top macaroni and cheese with bread crumb mixture. Bake casserole until golden brown and bubbly, about 30 minutes. Remove from oven and allow to rest about 10 minutes before serving.

Smoked Shrimp

This spicy Cajun-style shrimp dish is a tasty snack, but you can also serve it with Andouille sausage and bowtie pasta for a hearty meal. If you don't want to mess with mixing your own Cajun seasoning, you can substitute a little more than ¼ cup store-bought Cajun seasoning.

INGREDIENTS | SERVES 6

2 pounds raw large (31–35) shrimp, peeled and deveined

2 tablespoons olive oil

1½ teaspoons sweet paprika

½ teaspoon kosher or sea salt

½ teaspoon ground white pepper

½ teaspoon ground sage

½ teaspoon freshly ground black pepper

¼ teaspoon onion powder

¼ teaspoon garlic powder

¼ teaspoon dried thyme

¼ teaspoon dried oregano

¼ teaspoon ground red pepper

1. Set up smoker or grill for indirect cooking and preheat to medium-high. Use a smoke bomb (see instructions in Chapter 3) or a smoker box to generate smoke.

2. Pat shrimp dry with paper towels and place them in a plastic resealable bag. Place olive oil in the bag, seal, and shake to coat. Place remaining ingredients in a small bowl and stir to combine. Pour spice mix in the bag and work with your hands to coat the shrimp. Refrigerate for 30 minutes.

3. Place shrimp in a grill pan and place on the unheated side of the grill. Add smoke bomb or smoker box with wood chips. Close lid and cook until shrimp is cooked through (about 15 minutes). Remove from heat and serve immediately.

Smoked Shrimp Tacos with Cumin-Cilantro Sauce

Shrimp tacos are a great way to switch up the normal taco dinner. These are loaded with flavor and just enough heat to please the chili fanatics. If you don't like cabbage, use shredded lettuce in the tacos instead.

INGREDIENTS | SERVES 4

¼ cup plain low-fat yogurt

¾ teaspoon ground cumin, divided

2 tablespoons chopped fresh cilantro

1 pound raw medium (41–50) shrimp, peeled and deveined

1 tablespoon olive oil

1 clove garlic, minced

½ teaspoon chili powder

¼ teaspoon kosher or sea salt

¼ teaspoon chipotle powder

8 (8-inch) corn tortillas

2 cups shredded cabbage

1 cup diced tomatoes

2 avocados, pitted and sliced

1. In a small bowl, combine yogurt, ¼ teaspoon cumin, and cilantro. Refrigerate until ready to use.

2. Set up smoker or grill for indirect cooking and preheat to medium-high. Use a smoke bomb (see instructions in Chapter 3) or smoker box to generate smoke.

3. Pat shrimp dry with paper towels and place them in a plastic resealable bag. Place olive oil in the bag, seal, and shake to coat. Place garlic, ½ teaspoon cumin, chili powder, salt, and chipotle powder in a small bowl and stir to combine. Pour spice mix in the bag and work with your hands to coat the shrimp. Refrigerate for 30 minutes.

4. Place shrimp in a grill pan and place on the unheated side of the grill. Add smoke bomb or smoker box with wood chips. Close lid and cook until shrimp is cooked through (about 10 minutes).

5. Heat tortillas and fill each one with 5 shrimp, ½ cup cabbage, and ¼ cup tomato. Top with avocado slices and yogurt sauce. Serve immediately.

CHAPTER 10

Poultry

Whether it's chicken, turkey, capon, duck, pheasant, Cornish hen, or any other bird, poultry is one of the best meats to put on the smoker. For the most part, except maybe for duck, any recipe is easily adaptable to another bird. So if it says chicken, think turkey or Cornish hen. Let your imagination run wild. If you've struggled turning out moist poultry off your grill, give brining a try. The extra moisture brining gives your poultry will make it just a little more tolerant on the grill.

RECIPES

Smoked Whole Chicken

There is nothing prettier off the smoker than a perfectly smoked whole chicken. The beautifully browned skin looks fantastic on the table. If you're going to take the time to smoke one, go ahead and smoke two. You'll want leftovers.

INGREDIENTS | SERVES 4

1 whole (4–5 pound) chicken

4 cups Poultry or Pork Brine (see recipe in Chapter 5)

1 lemon with peel, roughly chopped

1 onion, peeled and roughly chopped

1 green apple, cored and roughly chopped

4 garlic cloves, peeled and quartered

2 teaspoons kosher or sea salt, divided

2 teaspoons freshly ground black pepper, divided

3 tablespoons olive oil, divided

3 tablespoons paprika

1. Place chicken in a large resealable plastic bag. Pour brine over chicken, making sure chicken is covered by at least 2 inches. Seal bag and brine chicken for 6 hours in refrigerator.

2. Remove chicken from brine and rinse completely, inside and out. Pat chicken dry and set aside.

3. Place lemon, onion, apple, and garlic in a large bowl. Add 1 teaspoon salt and 1 teaspoon pepper and mix to combine. Add 1 tablespoon olive oil and mix again. Stuff as much of the mixture into the cavities of the chicken as will fit. Fold the wings under to hold the skin in place. Tie legs together to hold large cavity closed.

4. Rub the entire chicken with the remaining olive oil. Mix 1 teaspoon salt, 1 teaspoon pepper, and paprika together and sprinkle lightly over the chicken.

5. If using a grill, set it up for indirect cooking. Preheat grill or smoker to medium-low, about 250°F.

6. If using a grill, place the chicken over the unheated side of the grill. Use a fruit wood to create smoke. Cook 3–5 hours, until the internal temperature of the thigh is 170°F. Remove from grill and let the chicken rest for 15 minutes before carving.

Bourbon-Brined and Smoked Chicken

If you don't want to use the bourbon brine, go ahead and give any other brine a try. Either way you're going to end up with great-tasting chicken.

INGREDIENTS | SERVES 4

1 whole (3–5 pound) chicken

6 cups Bourbon Chicken Brine (see recipe in Chapter 5)

Reserved lemon, garlic, onion, and apple from the Bourbon Chicken Brine

½ teaspoon freshly ground black pepper

1 tablespoon butter, melted

1. Place chicken in one or two large resealable plastic bags. Pour brine over chicken, making sure chicken is covered by at least 1 inch. Brine chicken for 6 hours in the refrigerator. Turn bag(s) over every hour.

2. Remove chicken from brine and rinse completely, inside and out. Pat chicken dry.

3. Stuff ½ of the lemon, garlic, onion, and apple into the cavities of the chicken. Fold the wings under to hold the skin in place. Tie legs together to hold large cavity closed.

4. If using a grill, set it up for indirect cooking. Preheat grill or smoker to medium-low, about 250°F.

5. If using a grill, place the chicken over the unheated side of the grill. Use a fruit wood to create smoke. Cook for 3–5 hours, until the internal temperature of the thigh is 170°F. Remove from grill and let the chicken rest for 15 minutes before carving.

Stovetop-Smoked Duck Breasts with Orange Sauce

Brining the duck breasts adds moisture to help ensure everything stays juicy. It also will help mask the natural gamey flavor that some people don't like about duck.

INGREDIENTS | SERVES 4

4 duck breasts, skin on

4 cups Basic Brine (see recipe in Chapter 5)

1½ cups chicken stock or duck stock

2 tablespoons orange marmalade

1 tablespoon Tabasco Green Jalapeño Sauce

2 ounces Cointreau or Grand Marnier orange liqueur

½ cup fresh orange juice, strained

1 tablespoon plus ⅛ teaspoon kosher or sea salt, divided

1 teaspoon freshly ground black pepper

1. Place duck breasts in a large resealable plastic bag. Pour brine over breasts, making sure they are covered by at least 2 inches. Seal bag and refrigerate for up to 8 hours. Remove breasts from brine, rinse, and allow them to rest for 1 hour before smoking.

2. While duck breasts are resting, pour the chicken stock into a large saucepan and heat over medium heat. Cook and reduce chicken/duck stock until you have ½ cup of highly reduced stock. This should take about an hour. The larger the surface area of the pot, the quicker the stock will reduce.

3. Set up stovetop smoker according to manufacturer's instructions. Smoke breasts on low heat for 30–45 minutes.

4. Combine marmalade, stock, jalapeño sauce, orange liqueur, orange juice, and ⅛ teaspoon salt in a small saucepan over low heat. Stir to combine. Simmer until thick, about 20 minutes.

5. Preheat oven to 450°F. Brush duck breasts with a thin layer of sauce; sprinkle with black pepper and remaining salt. Roast in the oven, skin side up, until the center of the breasts are a very light pink (about 15 minutes). You can use the rack and pan from your stovetop smoker to finish the duck breasts in the oven or use a medium ungreased baking dish or cast-iron skillet.

6. Allow breasts to rest 5 minutes and cut into ¼-inch slices. Serve with remaining orange sauce.

Smoked Pheasant

Brining and then smoking the pheasant will remove the gaminess that some people find unappealing. The maple syrup adds a nice sweet touch to the savory barbecue rub.

INGREDIENTS | SERVES 4

4 pheasants, around 2 pounds each

4 cups any brine (see recipes in Chapter 5)

¼ cup dry rub

2 cups Grade A maple syrup

1. Place pheasants in a large resealable plastic bag. Pour the brine over the pheasants, making sure they are covered by at least 1 inch of liquid. Seal bag and place in the refrigerator for at least 1 hour, but not more than 3 hours.

2. Remove pheasants from brine, rinse, and pat dry. Season with dry rub and set aside.

3. In a medium saucepan over medium heat, reduce the maple syrup to 1 cup of thick syrup (about 30 minutes).

4. Preheat cooker to 220°F with indirect heat. Smoke pheasant until done, when it's internal temperature is about 155°F degrees, about 2 hours. Brush with reduced maple syrup every 45 minutes after the first hour has passed. Remove from heat and serve immediately.

Smoked Turkey Legs

Do you want to replicate those giant turkey legs that are so popular at the state fair? This recipe should do the trick. For an added treat, save a couple legs, remove the meat, and use them for great-tasting sandwiches or a quick turkey hash on Saturday morning.

INGREDIENTS | SERVES 8

¼ cup soy sauce

2 tablespoons vegetable oil

8 turkey legs

¼ cup dry rub

1 cup vinegar-based barbecue mop

1 cup barbecue sauce

1. Set up smoker or grill for indirect heat cooking and preheat to 225°F.

2. Mix soy sauce and oil together in a small bowl. Whisk to blend. Rub soy sauce mixture over each turkey leg. Dust with dry rub. Rub it over and under the skin. Place legs in a resealable plastic bag and refrigerate for 2 hours.

3. Lay the turkey legs over the unheated side of the grill. The turkey legs should be laid as close as possible together without touching to allow for the heat and smoke to surround the whole leg. Smoke turkey legs until tender and juices run clear (about 3½–4 hours). Brush with mop every 45 minutes. Remove from heat when done, allow to rest 5 minutes, and serve with barbecue sauce on the side.

Smoked Chicken and Three-Cheese Ziti

This is a great way to use up leftover smoked chicken. You might even want to smoke an extra one just for this dish. The smoky flavor of the chicken is a great complement to all three cheeses.

INGREDIENTS | SERVES 8

12 ounces dried ziti pasta

3 tablespoons butter

2 cloves garlic, minced

3 tablespoons all-purpose flour

¼ teaspoon kosher or sea salt

¼ teaspoon ground white pepper

3½ cups whole milk

1½ cups finely shredded Asiago cheese

1 cup finely shredded fontina cheese

½ cup crumbled blue cheese

2 cups chopped smoked chicken

⅓ cup fine dry bread crumbs

2 teaspoons melted butter

1. Preheat oven to 375°F. Grease a 2-quart casserole; set aside.

2. Cook pasta according to package directions; drain. Return to pan.

3. In a large saucepan or Dutch oven over medium heat, melt 3 tablespoons butter. Add garlic and stir for 30 seconds or until you can smell the garlic aroma. Stir in the flour, salt, and white pepper.

4. Slowly add the milk, stirring constantly. Cook until thickened and bubbly, about 15 minutes. Add the cheeses a little at a time, stirring between batches until all the cheese is melted and blended together. Stir in the chicken and cooked pasta.

5. Carefully transfer the chicken and pasta mixture to the greased casserole. In a small bowl, mix together the bread crumbs and 2 teaspoons melted butter. Sprinkle bread crumb mixture over the top of the chicken and pasta. Bake at 375°F for 30 minutes or until heated through and bread crumbs have browned. Allow to rest 10 minutes before serving.

Pulled Chicken Sliders

Looking for a great game-time snack? You're going to love these little sandwiches! Not only are they simple to make, they're packed with a ton of flavor.

INGREDIENTS | SERVES 4

2 cups shredded leftover smoked chicken

8 small sweet Hawaiian dinner rolls

½ cup barbecue sauce

8 large dill or sweet pickle slices

Sweet Hawaiian Dinner Rolls

Hawaiian dinner rolls are a sweet dinner roll made popular by the King's Hawaiian Company. The soft and sweet rolls are perfect for making small pulled pork sliders.

1. Reheat shredded chicken. Cut dinner rolls in half and toast.

2. Place ¼ cup of shredded smoked chicken on top of each roll bottom. Top with 1 tablespoon of sauce and a pickle slice. Add top bun and serve.

Tea-Smoked Squab

This recipe uses a wok to smoke the squab in a traditional Chinese method. If you don't have a wok, you can make do with a cast-iron skillet, stovetop smoker, or just about any other smoking method mentioned in this book.

INGREDIENTS | SERVES 2

3 tablespoons dark soy sauce

2 tablespoons soy sauce

1 tablespoon sugar

2 teaspoons minced ginger

2 whole squabs

⅔ cup oolong or black tea leaves

⅓ cup long-grain rice

½ cup packed brown sugar

1 teaspoon Chinese five-spice powder

What Is a Squab?

A squab is a pigeon. Not your run-of-the-mill pigeon you see flying around the neighborhood, but one specially bred and raised for eating. They have a mild flavor and take smoke very well. However, if you can't get used to the idea of eating pigeon, you can substitute Cornish game hens or even small chickens.

1. Place soy sauces, sugar, and ginger in a large resealable plastic bag. Shake the bag to combine. Add squabs to the bag. Squeeze out as much air as possible and seal. Work sealed bag in your hands to coat the squabs. Refrigerate overnight.

2. Remove squabs from the marinade and pat dry. Using a stovetop steamer, bring a large pot of water to a boil over medium heat. Place dried squabs in steamer basket and insert into the water pot. Cover and reduce heat to low; steam the squabs for 25 minutes.

3. Completely line the inside of a wok and lid with foil. Mix the tea, rice, brown sugar, and five-spice powder in a small bowl. Spread the tea mixture evenly over the bottom of the wok on top of the foil. Place a round cake rack over the smoking ingredients. Place squabs on cake rack.

4. Over high heat, uncovered, heat the wok until smoke begins to appear. Cover wok with lid and reduce the heat to medium-low. Smoke for 8–10 minutes. Turn off the heat and, without removing the lid, allow to rest for 3 minutes before serving.

Smoked and Fried Chicken Wings

The traditional method for cooking chicken wings is to bake them before saucing and serving. This recipe adds two levels of flavor by first smoking the wings and then crisping the skin by quickly flash-frying them before saucing. You can spice these up any way you want. Try a 50/50 mixture of melted butter and barbecue sauce.

INGREDIENTS | SERVES 4

2 pounds chicken drumettes, thawed, rinsed, and patted dry

½ cup dry rub

6 cups vegetable oil

1 cup barbecue sauce

Want Some Big Wings?

For a treat, use turkey wings instead of chicken wings. Just increase the smoking time about 30–40 minutes, depending upon the size of the wings. Remember, time isn't the best way to tell if something is done. In the case of any poultry, double-check to make sure any juices are running clear.

1. Season the chicken drumettes liberally with dry rub. Allow to sit at room temperature for 10 minutes.

2. Line the inside and lid of a wok with foil. Place 1 cup of alder wood chips in the bottom of the wok. Insert a small round cake rack over the top of the chips. Turn heat on high. When smoke begins to appear, place the chicken on the cake rack and cover the wok. Reduce heat to medium-low.

3. Smoke the chicken drumettes for 1 hour or until juices run clear. Remove from wok and let rest for 5 minutes.

4. Heat oil in a large deep-sided frying pan to 350°F. Fry smoked chicken drumettes for 5 minutes or until skin turns a deep golden brown. Drain well on paper towels before tossing with the sauce. Serve immediately.

Smoked Chicken or Turkey Jerky

If you need a healthy, protein-filled snack for a road trip or camping, give chicken or turkey jerky a try. If poultry isn't your idea of jerky, you can also use beef.

INGREDIENTS | SERVES 6

2 pounds boneless, skinless chicken or turkey

½ teaspoon kosher or sea salt

1 tablespoon fresh ginger

½ teaspoon freshly ground black pepper

¼ cup sugar

½ cup soy sauce

1 large garlic clove, minced

Electric Smoker

Smoking jerky on a charcoal grill can be more challenging than using a gas grill. Ideally, if you are planning to make jerky on a frequent basis, it will be easier to purchase an electric smoker like the Masterbuilt or Bradley. They give you more control over the heat while still allowing for good smoke coverage.

1. Place chicken or turkey in the freezer for 45 minutes. Remove from freezer and slice into ⅛-inch slices.

2. Combine salt, ginger, pepper, sugar, soy sauce, and garlic in a resealable plastic bag. Add chicken or turkey slices. Squeeze as much air out of the bag as possible. Seal and refrigerate for no more than 4 hours, turning every 30 minutes.

3. Remove slices from the bag and discard marinade. Pat dry with paper towels.

4. Set up your gas grill for indirect cooking and preheat to low. Place the chicken or turkey slices on a wire rack. Place wire rack on the grill and cook for 1 hour at low temperature, about 140°F.

5. After an hour, slowly raise the temperature of the grill to 160°F and smoke, using a smoker box, for 3 hours.

6. Raise temperature to 185°F and continue to cook with or without smoke for another 2–3 hours, until the jerky has reduced in size by about 50 percent. The jerky should be dry, but not brittle.

Cupcake Tin Chicken Thighs

Chef Myron Mixon developed this technique to cook chicken for competitions. This is a nice way to smoke chicken, and it looks really cute on the plate too.

INGREDIENTS | SERVES 3

6 medium chicken thighs, bone-in and skin on

3 tablespoons dry rub

3¼ cups chicken stock

½ cup barbecue sauce

1. Place the chicken thighs, skin side down, on a cutting board. With a cleaver or shears, remove the knuckle from each thigh bone. Trim the thigh meat, but not the skin, so the thigh is about 3 inches across. Cut the skin so it is ¼ inch bigger than the meat all the way around. Each thigh should be about 3 inches across when trimming is complete.

2. Set up your smoker or grill for indirect cooking and preheat to medium-high. Use whatever smoke-generating method works best for you.

3. Season the thighs with dry rub. Place thighs, skin side down, into a greased cupcake pan. Place the cupcake pan into a slightly larger aluminum foil pan. Pour chicken stock into the foil pan, being careful not to get any on the chicken.

4. Place the pan on the smoker and cook for 90 minutes at 300°F. After 90 minutes, remove pans from the smoker. To keep the chicken from sticking to the baking sheet, use parchment paper or spray the sheet with nonstick cooking spray. Flip the chicken thighs out onto a baking sheet. Return to the smoker for another 45 minutes.

5. Brush thighs with sauce and place back on smoker for 40 minutes. Remove from smoker and serve.

Teriyaki Chicken Skewers

Chicken on a stick is fun to eat. These skewers are great to serve during the summer months when you want something light.

INGREDIENTS | SERVES 10

2 pounds boneless, skinless chicken thighs

1 (6-ounce) can pineapple juice

¼ cup vegetable oil

¼ cup soy sauce

3 tablespoons brown sugar

½ teaspoon garlic powder

6 tablespoons sesame oil

¼ teaspoon minced garlic

1 lemon, juiced

1 teaspoon freshly ground black pepper

30 (8-inch) bamboo skewers

1 tablespoon sesame seeds, toasted

1. Cut chicken into 1-inch slices.

2. Mix the pineapple juice, vegetable oil, soy sauce, brown sugar, garlic powder, seasame oil, garlic, lemon juice, and pepper. Pour marinade into a resealable plastic bag along with the chicken. Squeeze as much air out of the bag as possible and seal. Work chicken with your hands to make sure all the chicken is coated. Refrigerate for at least 2 hours.

3. Soak bamboo skewers in water for at least 1 hour. Set up grill for direct heat cooking and preheat to medium.

4. Thread 1 chicken slice on each skewer. Place chicken skewers on a wire rack. Toss 1 cup of dry wood chips on the heat source. Quickly place the rack with skewers on it onto the grill and close the lid. Cook until internal temperature reaches 165°F (about 30 minutes). Remove from grill and garnish with toasted seasame seeds. Serve immediately.

Smoked Chicken and Navy Bean Chili

This easy dish can be made very quickly if you have leftover smoked chicken around. Serve this chili with avocados, sour cream, cilantro, and anything else you want on the side.

INGREDIENTS | SERVES 8

¾ pound boneless, skinless chicken breasts, cut into 1-inch cubes

½ teaspoon kosher or sea salt

¼ teaspoon freshly ground black pepper

2 tablespoons olive oil

1 medium onion, chopped

4 garlic cloves, minced

1 jalapeño pepper, seeded and chopped

2 teaspoons dried oregano

1 teaspoon ground cumin

2 (15-ounce) cans white kidney or cannellini beans, drained and rinsed

3 cups chicken broth

4 cups shredded Cheddar cheese

1. Set stovetop smoker up according to manufacturer's directions. Season chicken with salt and pepper. Add 3 tablespoons wood dust to smoker. Place chicken on rack in smoker and place smoker on the stove. Turn burner on medium heat. When smoke starts to appear, close smoker, reduce heat to low, and smoke for about 20 minutes. Remove chicken from smoker and set aside.

2. Heat oil in a Dutch oven over medium-high heat and sauté the onion, garlic, and jalapeño for 2 minutes. Stir in oregano and cumin and cook for about 1 minute more or until the vegetables are tender.

3. Add chicken, beans, and chicken broth to the sautéed vegetables. Bring to a boil, then reduce heat to low. Simmer for 30 minutes. Remove ½ cup of beans from chili and mash until smooth. Return to Dutch oven and gently stir to mix.

4. Divide chili into 8 bowls and top each with ½ cup cheese.

Smoked Chicken Salad

A chicken salad is great way to use smoked chicken. You can serve the salad on a a bed of mixed greens or make a sandwich out of it.

INGREDIENTS | SERVES 6

3 cups chopped skinless, boneless chicken breasts

⅛ teaspoon kosher or sea salt

⅛ teaspoon freshly ground black pepper

¼ cup plain fat-free yogurt

¼ cup light mayonnaise

1 teaspoon Dijon mustard

⅓ cup chopped green onions

¼ cup chopped smoked almonds

1 teaspoon chopped fresh rosemary

Salad or Sandwich

The great thing about a good smoked chicken is that it not only makes a great sandwich, but adding it to some spring mix or lettuce along with sliced tomatoes makes for an equally delicious salad.

1. Set up stovetop smoker according to manufacturer's directions.

2. Season chicken with salt and pepper. Add 3 tablespoons wood dust to smoker. Place chicken on rack in smoker and place on the stove. Turn burner on medium heat. When smoke starts to appear, close smoker, reduce heat to low, and smoke for about 40 minutes. Remove from the smoker and cool to room temperature. Refrigerate for at least 1 hour.

3. In a medium bowl, combine yogurt, mayonnaise, mustard, green onions, almonds, and rosemary. Stir or whisk to mix well. Add chicken and fold gently until combined. Refrigerate for 20 minutes before serving.

CHAPTER 11

Side Dishes

While meat may be the main attraction for a barbecued meal, there are a multitude of side dishes available that are not only easy to make, but will complement and even enhance the flavor of your smoked meat. Even though there are some side-dish staples like cornbread and beans, don't be afraid to mix and match flavors. Your guests will love the variety of options they have, and you'll get some great practice with your smoker.

RECIPES

Tangy and Creamy Cole Slaw

Malt vinegar gives this dish a slightly nutty, toasty flavor that works well with most smoked foods.
Serve as a side dish for pork or seafood.

INGREDIENTS | SERVES 6

8 cups shredded cabbage

2 tablespoons malt vinegar

⅔ cup mayonnaise

2 teaspoons sugar

2 teaspoons yellow mustard

1. Place shredded cabbage in large bowl.

2. In small bowl, whisk remaining ingredients together.

3. Pour dressing over cabbage and mix lightly. Refrigerate for 30 minutes before serving.

Carolina Pulled Pork Sandwich Slaw

If you've never put coleslaw inside your pulled pork sandwich, you don't know what you're missing!
The vinegar and mayonnaise complement the smokiness of the pork perfectly.

INGREDIENTS | SERVES 6

2 cups shredded cabbage

2 tablespoons minced onions

2 tablespoons white vinegar

1½ tablespoons mayonnaise

2 teaspoons sugar

¼ teaspoon kosher or sea salt

¼ teaspoon freshly ground black pepper

1. Place cabbage in a large bowl.

2. In a small bowl, combine the remaining ingredients and stir to blend.

3. Pour dressing mixture over cabbage and gently stir to combine. Refrigerate for 30 minutes before serving.

Sweet Potato Cornbread

This is not your everyday cornbread. The addition of the sweet potato adds a level of moisture and flavor you don't usually find in cornbread, and the pumpkin pie spice is a great addition if you are making this as a holiday treat.

INGREDIENTS | SERVES 6

1 cup cooked, mashed sweet potato

2 large eggs, lightly beaten

3 tablespoons packed brown sugar

1¼ cups buttermilk

¼ cup vegetable oil

1½ cups white corn meal

½ cup all-purpose flour

2 teaspoons baking powder

½ teaspoon kosher or sea salt

1 teaspoon pumpkin pie spice

Sugar or No Sugar

Whether to add sugar to cornbread is a big decision for cornbread experts. For example, if you're in the southern part of the United States and add sugar to your cornbread, you're not making bread, you're baking a cake.

1. Preheat oven to 375°F.

2. Generously coat a 10½-inch cast-iron skillet with nonstick cooking spray. Preheat skillet in the oven for 10 minutes.

3. In a large mixing bowl, stir together sweet potato, eggs, brown sugar, buttermilk, and oil. Blend until smooth. Stir in cornmeal, flour, baking powder, salt, and pumpkin pie spice until well blended. Pour batter into hot skillet.

4. Bake for 45 minutes or until a toothpick comes out clean when inserted into the middle of the cornbread.

Texas Ranch Beans

If you're looking for the perfect complement to anything off the smoker, this bean dish is it. For a complete meal, pour a heaping ladle of these tasty beans over a hunk of Sweet Potato Cornbread (see recipe in this chapter). These beans are better if prepared the day before serving.

INGREDIENTS | SERVES 6

1 pound dried pinto beans

1 (8-ounce) can tomato sauce

1 tablespoon kosher or sea salt

1 tablespoon sugar

1 tablespoon ground cumin

1 teaspoon freshly ground black pepper

1 tablespoon chili powder

4 beef bouillon cubes

2 tablespoons bacon drippings

2 medium onions, chopped

1 (4–5-inch) link smoked sausage, sliced

Rocks and Beans

It's always a good idea to carefully go through your dried beans to remove any broken beans, rocks, or dirt. As careful as the packagers are, there is always a chance some rocks and dirt ended up in the package.

1. Sort and rinse beans thoroughly. Place beans in large bowl with water to cover. Add tomato sauce, salt, sugar, cumin, pepper, chili powder, and bouillon cubes. Soak beans overnight, stirring occasionally.

2. Heat bacon drippings in a heavy Dutch oven over medium-high heat. Sauté onions and sausage for 8–10 minutes.

3. Pour in bean mixture and bring to a boil. Reduce heat to low, cover, and simmer for approximately 8 hours. The beans should be covered by ¼ inch of liquid during the entire cooking time. Stir occasionally, and add additional water if necessary.

4. During the last 2 hours, mash some of the beans against the side of pot to thicken the cooking liquid.

Southern-Style Collard Greens

When cooked to tender perfection with the added bonus of a smoked ham hock, collard greens is the ideal Southern side dish. Don't forget to serve it with a little vinegar and hot sauce on the side for an extra zing.

INGREDIENTS | SERVES 6

2 tablespoons bacon fat

1 medium onion, peeled and sliced ¼-inch thick

1 smoked ham hock

2 garlic cloves, smashed

1 quart chicken broth

2 cups water

8–10 cups chopped collard greens

Greens and More Greens

Collards are one the most popular greens, but don't be afraid to try others. Mustard greens along with turnip, beet, and radish tops also make a great addition to the collards. You can toss in a little kale, too.

1. In a Dutch oven over medium-high heat, melt bacon fat. Sauté onions until the edges just begin to brown, stirring frequently, about 5 minutes.

2. Add the ham hock, garlic, chicken broth, and water to the pot and bring to a simmer. Reduce heat to low, cover, and cook for 1 hour.

3. Add the collard greens and cook another 45 minutes or until the collard greens are tender.

4. Remove ham hock from the pot. Let cool slightly and remove all the meat from the hock. Chop the meat and return it to the pot.

Smoked Macaroni and Cheese

Macaroni and cheese is a always a crowd pleaser. If you don't like sharp Cheddar cheese, substitute medium-sharp cheese or use a combination of different cheeses. If you want to add a little smoke flavor, use some cold-smoked cheese.

INGREDIENTS | SERVES 6

8 ounces dry elbow macaroni

½ pound extra-sharp Cheddar cheese, cut into ½-inch cubes

2 tablespoons plus 1 teaspoon flour

1½ teaspoon dry mustard

¼ teaspoon freshly ground black pepper

¼ teaspoon freshly grated nutmeg

⅛ teaspoon cayenne pepper

½ teaspoon kosher or sea salt

⅔ cup sour cream

2 eggs, lightly beaten

1½ cups half-and-half

1½ cups heavy cream

⅓ cup grated onion

1 teaspoon Worcestershire sauce

2 cups shredded extra-sharp Cheddar cheese

1. Preheat smoker to 350°F.

2. Bring a large pot of salted water to a boil. Add pasta and cook about 3 minutes. The pasta should be only half-cooked. Drain pasta and transfer to a greased 9" × 13" baking dish. Stir in the cubed Cheddar cheese and set aside.

3. In a large bowl, stir together the flour, mustard, black pepper, nutmeg, cayenne, and salt. Add sour cream and eggs and whisk until smooth. Whisk in the half-and-half, heavy cream, onion, and Worcestershire sauce. Pour mixture over the pasta and cheese mixture and stir to combine. Sprinkle the grated cheese evenly over the top.

4. Smoke for about 30 minutes or until cheese starts to brown on the edges. Allow to cool 10 minutes before serving.

Hasselback Potatoes with Herb Sour Cream

This dish is rustic enough for the picnic table or fancy enough for the dining room. It can be cooked in the oven, on the grill, or in the smoker.

INGREDIENTS | SERVES 6

½ cup sour cream

½ teaspoon garlic powder

1 tablespoon finely chopped fresh parsley

1¼ teaspoons kosher or sea salt, divided

1¼ teaspoons freshly ground black pepper, divided

1 pound medium red new potatoes

5 garlic cloves, thinly sliced

4 tablespoons unsalted butter, melted

2 tablespoons olive oil

Wooden Spoon Cradle

To make cutting the slits in the potatoes a little easier and safer, place each potato in the bowl of a wooden spoon to help hold it in place.

1. Combine the sour cream, garlic powder, parsley, ¼ teaspoon salt, and ¼ teaspoon pepper in a small bowl. Refrigerate for 30 minutes.

2. Preheat oven to 400°F.

3. Carefully cut parallel slits, about ¼ inch apart, from one end of each potato to the other. Slices should go almost all the way through the potato.

4. Place a garlic slice between slits at the crown of each potato. Carefully toss potatoes in a medium bowl with butter and olive oil.

5. Place potatoes on an ungreased baking sheet and sprinkle with the remaining salt and pepper. Bake for 1 hour or until the tops are crispy and the potatoes are cooked all the way through. Transfer to a platter and top with the sour cream mixture.

Roasted Asparagus Wrapped in Prosciutto

It doesn't get much better than asparagus wrapped in Italian bacon. Not only can you cook this dish the day before serving, but it's probably better if you do. For a little extra flavor and color, grill the asparagus stalks instead of roasting them.

INGREDIENTS | SERVES 4

1 pound asparagus, trimmed

1 tablespoon olive oil

1 teaspoon kosher or sea salt

1 teaspoon freshly ground black pepper

8 thin slices prosciutto, halved lengthwise

1. Preheat the oven to 400°F.

2. Place asparagus in a single layer on a baking sheet. Drizzle with olive oil, salt, and pepper. Toss to coat. Roast asparagus about 15 minutes or until tender. Cool to room temperature.

3. Wrap each stalk of asparagus in half a slice of prosciutto, leaving the tips exposed. Serve at room temperature.

Hint of Heat Carrot Salad

The sambal oelek adds a different type of heat to this carrot that matches perfectly with the natural sweetness of the carrots. Adding the mint and cilantro makes this a great salad for hot afternoons at the park or on the patio.

INGREDIENTS | SERVES 4

3 tablespoons extra-virgin olive oil

1 tablespoon fresh lemon juice

1 teaspoon sambal oelek (ground fresh chile paste)

4 cups coarsely grated carrot (about 1 pound)

½ teaspoon kosher or sea salt

2 tablespoons chopped fresh cilantro

1 tablespoon minced fresh mint

1 tablespoon minced fresh chives

1. Combine olive oil, lemon juice, and sambal oelek in a large bowl and whisk until well blended. Add carrots and salt. Toss to coat. Let stand 30 minutes.

2. Add cilantro, mint, and chives. Toss ingredients together and serve at room temperature or chilled.

Sambal Oelek

Sambal oelek is an Indonesian chili sauce made from ground raw chilies. *Oelek* is the dutch spelling for the Indonesian word *ulek*. A ulek is a stone mortar traditionally used to grind the chilies.

Sweet Potato Fries

Sweet potatoe fries go with just about any smoked meat. A plate of sweet potato fries with a pile of pulled pork or chopped brisket on top and then drizzled with barbecue sauce is great appetizer or maybe even a meal.

INGREDIENTS | SERVES 6

5 sweet potatoes, peeled and cut into ¼-inch strips

2 tablespoons vegetable oil

1 tablespoon any dry rub (see recipes in Chapter 5)

½ teaspoon hot smoked paprika

1. Preheat oven to 450°F. Line a baking sheet with parchment paper.

2. In a large bowl, toss sweet potatoes with oil to coat. Sprinkle with rub and paprika and toss again. Spread potatoes in single layer on prepared baking sheet.

3. Bake until sweet potatoes are tender and golden brown (about 20 minutes), turning occasionally. Let cool 5–10 minutes before serving.

Carrot and Apple Slaw

This refreshing, crunchy slaw is a great side dish and a surprising addition to pulled pork sandwiches.

INGREDIENTS | SERVES 8

½ cup sour cream

2 tablespoons white wine vinegar

½ teaspoon ground cumin

½ teaspoon kosher or sea salt

¼ teaspoon freshly ground black pepper

¾ pound carrots, peeled and grated

2 large Granny Smith apples, cored, peeled, and shredded

½ cup golden raisins

¼ cup chopped fresh cilantro

Combine all ingredients in a large bowl. Refrigerate for 20 minutes before serving.

Smoked Beans

Place the beans in the smoker while you're smoking your meats and they will both be ready at the same time. Cook the beans a day or two prior to your planned meal and they'll be even better. Make sure you allow the beans to cool completely before storing them in a covered container in the refrigerator.

INGREDIENTS | SERVES 6

4 slices bacon, cut into ½-inch pieces

1 onion, peeled and chopped

1 teaspoon kosher or sea salt

1 teaspoon freshly ground black pepper

1 pound dried navy beans, soaked in water overnight and drained

½ cup molasses

¼ cup ketchup

1 tablespoon dry mustard

5 cups water

2 tablespoons cider vinegar

1. Set up smoker or grill for indirect heat and heat to 250°F.

2. In a Dutch oven over medium heat, cook the bacon until crisp (about 5–6 minutes). Add onion, salt, and pepper. Cook another 5 minutes or until onions are tender.

3. Add beans, molasses, ketchup, mustard, and 5 cups of water and stir to combine. Bring to a boil.

4. Place Dutch oven in the smoker or grill, covered. Smoke for about 2 hours. Uncover and smoke, stirring every 15 minutes until thickened, for about 1½ hours. Stir in vinegar and serve.

Smoked and Grilled Corn with Cilantro

Grilled corn on the cob is the perfect summer side dish—it works well with any barbecue meal.

INGREDIENTS | SERVES 4

4 large ears corn, shucked and cut in half

2 tablespoons olive oil

1 teaspoon kosher or sea salt

1 teaspoon freshly ground black pepper

½ cup chopped fresh cilantro

2 teaspoons fresh lime juice, plus lime wedges for serving

1. Set up grill for direct heat cooking and preheat to medium-high.

2. In a large bowl, toss corn cob halves in oil and season with salt and pepper. Toss 1 cup of dry wood chips on the heat source and grill the corn uncovered until tender (about 12 minutes). Turn occasionally to get char marks over all sides of the corn.

3. Return corn to the same bowl you used to toss before. Add cilantro and lime juice and toss to coat the corn. Serve immediately with lime wedges on the side.

Smoked Corn Pudding

If you want to add even more smoky goodness to this dish, grill fresh corn on the cob. Remove the kernels from the cob and use that instead of frozen corn.

INGREDIENTS | SERVES 6

6 tablespoons unsalted butter, divided

1 medium onion, peeled and chopped

1¼ teaspoon kosher or sea salt, divided

½ teaspoon freshly ground black pepper, divided

2 cups heavy cream

5 large eggs

¼ cup all-purpose flour

2 tablespoons sugar

3 cups frozen corn, divided

1. Set up grill or smoker for indirect heat cooking and preheat to high heat. Spray an 8-inch baking dish with nonstick cooking spray.

2. In a small skillet over medium heat, melt 3 tablespoons butter. Add onion, ¼ teaspoon salt, and ¼ teaspoon pepper. Cook, stirring occasionally, until onion is softened (about 8 minutes).

3. Combine cream, eggs, flour, sugar, 2 cups corn, and the remaining butter, salt, and pepper in a blender or food processor. Blend until smooth. Add cooked onion and remaining corn; pulse once. Pour the mixture into the prepared baking dish.

4. Place on smoker, add smoke bomb (see instructions in Chapter 3) or smoker box, and cook until set but sort of jiggly in the middle (about 1 hour).

Macaroni Salad

There are some basic side dishes that are just too good to pass up. Macaroni salad is one of them.
Add ¾ pound cubed smoked chicken to turn this side dish into a main entrée.

INGREDIENTS | SERVES 6

¾ cup mayonnaise

2 tablespoons fresh lemon juice

½ teaspoon kosher or sea salt

¼ teaspoon freshly ground black pepper

3 cups cooked elbow macaroni, chilled

2 large hard-boiled eggs, peeled and chopped

2 green onions, thinly sliced

4 stalks celery, chopped

¼ cup chopped fresh flat-leaf parsley

1. In a large bowl, whisk together mayonnaise, lemon juice, salt, and pepper.

2. Fold in the macaroni, eggs, green onions, celery, and parsley. Chill until ready to serve.

CHAPTER 12

Meatless Menu Items

Just because it isn't meat doesn't mean it can't be cooked in your smoker! One of the great aspects of adding wood smoke flavor to foods is that it elevates the flavors for both meat eaters and meatless eaters. You'll be amazed at what kinds of foods you can smoke, from cheese to vegetables to tofu and beyond. Try using a variety of sauces to enhance the flavor of these dishes even more.

RECIPES

Smoked Summer Vegetable Kebabs

Using skewers for kebabs makes it easier to turn over the veggies while they are cooking. You can serve the cooked vegetables on the skewers or remove and serve them family-style from a big bowl or platter.

INGREDIENTS | SERVES 12

¼ cup dry white wine

¼ cup honey

3 garlic cloves, minced

2 tablespoons balsamic vinegar

2 tablespoons olive oil

1½ teaspoons pepper

1 teaspoon kosher or sea salt

16 cups assorted cut vegetables (see following table for size guidelines)

Grilled Antipasto

Grilled vegetables make a wonderful antipasto. Cool them to room temperature or chill in the refrigerator. Serve vegetables on a platter with assorted cheeses, olives, and crackers.

1. If using wooden or bamboo skewers, soak them in water for a minimum of 30 minutes.

2. In a large bowl, whisk the wine, honey, garlic, vinegar, oil, pepper, and salt together until blended. Remove ¼ cup.

3. Add vegetables to the remaining wine mixture. Cover and refrigerate for 30 minutes to 2 hours. Drain marinade from vegetables. Discard marinade.

4. Set up grill for direct heat cooking and preheat to 375°F.

5. Thread vegetables, with cut sides facing in the same direction, onto skewers. Thread each skewer with one type of vegetable. Grill using either a smoker box or smoke bomb (see instructions in Chapter 3) to create smoke flavor. See the following table for cooking times. Green onions and asparagus have been included, but you can put them directly on the grates.

6. Remove skewers from grill and place on a platter for serving. If desired, remove the vegetables from the skewers. Drizzle with reserved wine mixture and serve immediately.

▼ VEGETABLE KEBAB SMOKING CHART

Vegetable	Size	Cooking Time
Summer squash	¾-inch slices	8–9 minutes per side
Japanese eggplant	¾-inch slices	6 minutes per side
Italian eggplant	¾-inch slices, quartered	6–8 minutes per side
Bell peppers	1-inch-wide strips	5–6 minutes per side
Cherry tomatoes	Use double skewers	4 minutes per side
Onions	Wedges	3–4 minutes per side
Mushrooms	Whole	4–5 minutes per side
Potatoes	¼-inch slices, halved	8 minutes per side
Green onions*	Trim both ends	5 minutes
Asparagus*	Trim both ends	5–6 minutes per side

*Grill without skewers

Smoked Tofu

The flavor of smoked tofu just might fool the meat eaters in your house. Smoking tofu is also a great way for people who don't like eating meat to enjoy a barbecue.

INGREDIENTS | SERVES 4

1 (12.3-ounce) block extra-firm tofu, drained and cut into 3 slices

1. Place two towels (cloth or paper) on a bowl, plate, or baking sheet. Place tofu on towels. Cover tofu with two additional layers of towel, then an additional bowl, plate, or baking sheet. Place something heavy like books or canned goods on top. Set aside to drain there for at least 30 minutes.

2. Cold smoke (under 90°F) the tofu for 50 minutes or until you have a nice, rich brown color. The texture is also important to check. You want the tofu to still have some give to it when pressed. Ideally, 45–50 minutes is enough smoke without drying it out.

3. Let the tofu rest a few minutes after smoking.

Smoked Tofu and Quinoa Salad

This entrée salad is a healthier way to add the taste of smoke to your diet.

INGREDIENTS | SERVES 4

¼ cup lemon juice

3 tablespoons extra-virgin olive oil

2 cloves garlic, minced

1 teaspoon kosher or sea salt

1 teaspoon freshly ground black pepper

6 ounces Smoked Tofu, diced (see recipe in this chapter)

3 cups cooked quinoa

1 yellow bell pepper, seeded and diced

1 cup halved grape tomatoes

1 cup diced English cucumber

1 cup diced avocado

½ cup chopped fresh Italian parsley

½ cup chopped fresh cilantro

Add lemon juice, oil, garlic, salt, and pepper to a medium bowl. Whisk ingredients to blend. Add remaining ingredients and toss to combine.

Take It with a Grain of Thought

Quinoa is a grain-like crop that is closer to beetroots, spinach, and tumbleweeds than to something like rice or couscous. It is gluten-free and very high in protein. While it may look like pasta, it is technically a seed.

Smoked Tofu Po' Boy with Spicy Remoulade

A meatless po' boy is the perfect dish for the vegetarians in your house. With the spicy remoulade, you'll have all the flavor you'd expect from this classic New Orleans sandwich.

INGREDIENTS | SERVES 4

1¼ cups mayonnaise

¼ cup stone-ground mustard

1 clove garlic, smashed

1 tablespoon pickle juice

1 tablespoon capers

1 teaspoon prepared horseradish

¼ teaspoon cayenne pepper

¼ teaspoon hot paprika

½ teaspoon hot sauce

½ cup flour

2 teaspoons smoked paprika

1 teaspoon cumin

1 teaspoon garlic salt

½ teaspoon fresh ground black pepper

1 cup cornstarch

1 cup cold water

⅓ cup cornmeal

⅔ cup fine bread crumbs

3 cups peanut oil

2 cups ½-inch cubed smoked tofu

4 (6-inch) hoagie rolls

4 romaine lettuce leaves

1. To make the remoulade, blend mayonnaise, mustard, garlic, pickle juice, capers, horseradish, cayenne, hot paprika, and hot sauce in a food processor until smooth. Spoon into a small bowl, cover, and refrigerate.

2. Mix flour with smoked paprika, cumin, garlic salt, and black pepper and place in a shallow dish. Make a slurry by mixing cornstarch with cold water in another shallow dish. In a third dish, combine cornmeal and bread crumbs.

3. Heat peanut oil in a large, deep frying pan to 375°F.

4. Working in batches, dredge tofu cubes in flour, then the cornstarch slurry, and finally the cornmeal mixture.

5. Fry tofu in hot oil until a golden brown, about 5 minutes per side. Drain on a wire rack or paper towels. Cover to keep warm while the other batches are fried.

6. Cut each hoagie roll in half diagonally. Slather a good amount of remoulade inside each hoagie half. Lay a leaf of lettuce in the bread and fill with fried smoked tofu. Serve hot.

Smoked Tomato Sauce

Try this versatile tomato sauce on pizza, over pasta, or with grilled vegetables.

INGREDIENTS | SERVES 4

8 medium-size ripe tomatoes, cored
8 cloves garlic
¼ teaspoon chipotle chili in adobo
2 tablespoons unsalted butter, softened
½ teaspoon kosher or sea salt
½ teaspoon freshly ground black pepper
⅛ teaspoon balsamic vinegar

1. Set up grill for indirect heat and preheat to medium-hot. Fill a smoker box or make a smoke bomb (see instructions in Chapter 3) using heavy-duty foil with two cups of smoke wood chips.

2. Place the tomatoes, cored side up, into a disposable foil cake pan, packing as tightly as possible. Place one garlic clove inside each tomato.

3. When grill is hot, place pan with tomatoes on the cool side of the grill. Set the smoker box or smoke bomb on the hot coals. With all the vents open, close the grill lid. Smoke for 60 minutes or until the tomatoes have begun to char and are shriveled. Check the heat and add charcoal if necessary. Replace wood chips if you need to. Remove tomatoes from the grill and allow to cool for a few minutes.

4. Transfer the tomatoes, garlic, and juices from the pan into a food processor and blend until smooth. Add chipotle and blend again. Strain mixture through a medium sieve or cheesecloth. Make sure you squeeze all the juice out of the solids.

5. Place tomato sauce into a medium saucepan over medium heat and bring to a simmer. Stir in butter, salt, pepper, and balsamic vinegar.

Stovetop-Smoked Root Vegetables

Use these tasty vegetable cubes as a side or main dish, or drop them into a soup for some added flavor and texture.

INGREDIENTS | SERVES 4

1 cup quartered small red potatoes

1 cup diced carrot

1 cup diced turnips, parsnips, or other root vegetable

1 large onion, peeled and cut into wedges

2 tablespoons olive oil

1 tablespoon dry rub

Freeze the Goodness

The vegetables in this recipe can be frozen for an easy side dish later on. To freeze, lay the smoked vegetable cubes in a single layer on a waxed paper–covered baking sheet. Let cool to room temperature, then put the whole baking sheet in the freezer for 2 hours. Once frozen, place vegetables in a resealable plastic bag and store in the freezer until you're ready to use them.

1. Set up stovetop smoker according to manufacturer's directions. Cover inside with foil. Spray foil with nonstick cooking spray.

2. In a medium bowl, combine all the vegetables. Add olive oil and stir to coat. Place vegetables in the smoker and sprinkle with dry rub.

3. Place smoker on the stove or grill over medium heat with lid on, but not closed. When smoke starts to show, close the lid completely and smoke for about 30 minutes or until the vegetables are tender.

Smoke-Grilled Eggplant with Orange-and-Lime Miso Sauce

If you're looking for a flavorful Asian-inspired vegetable recipe, look no further than this recipe. The combination of citrus and miso will make this a great dish to serve with sticky rice or maybe some steamed buns.

INGREDIENTS | SERVES 6

3 tablespoons miso

1 tablespoon honey

2 tablespoons mirin

2 tablespoons water

¼ cup orange juice

¼ cup lime juice

1 tablespoon finely minced fresh ginger

4 Japanese eggplants, sliced lengthwise

1. In a small saucepan over medium heat, combine all ingredients except eggplant. Bring to a simmer, stirring frequently. Remove from heat and cool.

2. Fill a smoker box or make a smoke bomb (see instructions in Chapter 3) using heavy-duty foil with two cups of smoke wood chips. Smoke eggplant for 3–4 minutes per side, basting with sauce twice.

Smoked Acorn Squash Soup

The acorn squash isn't quite as popular as its cousin, the butternut squash, but it's packed with great flavor that is brightened by the delicate flavor of smoke. If you've got a meat eater who won't give this vegetable a try, toss in a few bacon crumbles at the end. Any winter squash will work with this recipe.

INGREDIENTS | SERVES 8

4 acorn squash, halved and seeded

1 cup melted butter

1 quart water, divided

1 quart vegetable stock

1 tablespoon teaspoon kosher or sea salt

1 tablespoon cumin

1 cup chopped fresh parsley

1 tablespoon paprika

¼ teaspoon cayenne pepper

4 cups sour cream

2 cups chopped fresh cilantro

1. Prepare grill for indirect heat cooking. Preheat to medium-hot. Place 2 fist-size chunks of hardwood on charcoal or gas burners.

2. When smoke begins to appear, reduce heat to medium-low and place squash halves, cut side down, on the cool side of the grill. Smoke the squash for 2 hours or until tender. Remove squash from grill and cool, uncovered.

3. Scoop out the flesh of the squash and transfer to a food processor. Add butter and 2 cups water to the food processor and blend until smooth. Transfer squash mixture to a stock pot. Stir in the remaining water and vegetable broth and heat over low heat. When soup begins to simmer, add salt, cumin, parsley, paprika, and cayenne. Simmer for 40 minutes.

4. To serve, ladle soup into bowls and serve with sour cream and cilantro on the side.

Smoked Spaghetti Squash with Smoked Tomato Sauce

Smoke gives spaghetti squash the appearance of whole wheat pasta. Cooking it on the grill brings out the natural nuttiness of the squash, which matches quite well with the smokiness of the tomatoes in the sauce.

INGREDIENTS | SERVES 4

1 spaghetti squash, halved and seeded

2 cups Smoked Tomato Sauce (see recipe in this chapter)

1 teaspoon Italian seasoning

2 tablespoons shredded Parmesan cheese

1. Prepare your grill for indirect heat cooking. Preheat to medium-hot. Place 2 fist-size chunks of hardwood on charcoal or gas burners.

2. When smoke begins to appear, reduce heat to medium-low and place squash halves, cut side down, on the cool side of the grill. Smoke the squash for 2 hours or until tender. Remove squash from grill and rest for 5 minutes. Use a fork to scrape the flesh from inside each squash half.

3. Combine the Smoked Tomato Sauce and Italian seasoning in a medium saucepan over low heat. Cook for 10 minutes, stirring occasionally.

4. To serve, place the spaghetti squash on a platter and top with Smoked Tomato Sauce. Garnish with Parmesan cheese.

Smoked Cauliflower with Chipotle Chili

There are so many things you can do with smoked cauliflower, you just might wonder why you didn't try before. Use the cauliflower as a side dish or crumble it onto a salad. You can even make a smoked cauliflower hummus out of it.

INGREDIENTS | SERVES 6

1 (2-pound) head cauliflower, green leaves trimmed off

¾ cup extra-virgin olive oil

¼ cup freshly squeezed lemon juice, from about 4 lemons

3 teaspoons ground chipotle chili pepper

5 tablespoons chopped cilantro leaves

1 teaspoon kosher or sea salt

Smoked Cauliflower Hummus

After grilling the cauliflower slices, allow them to cool. Crumble the cauliflower into a food processor and blend with 1 clove garlic, ⅓ cup tahini, 2 tablespoons lemon juice, and 2 tablespoons olive oil until smooth. If it is too thick, add 1 tablespoon of water at a time until you get the consistency you desire.

1. Line a large wok and lid with foil. Place 1 cup of oak wood chips in the bottom of the wok. Place a round cake rack over the wood chips. Turn heat to medium until smoke starts to appear. Place cauliflower head on cake rack and close the lid. Reduce heat to as low as you can while maintaining enough heat to keep chips smoking. Smoke cauliflower for 45 minutes or until fork tender. Remove from wok and cool slightly.

2. Set up grill for direct heat cooking and preheat to high.

3. With the cauliflower on a cutting board, cut the whole head into about 8–10 slices. Brush oil onto both sides of each slice. Transfer the slices to the grill directly over the coals and grill for about 3 minutes per side, until they are lightly charred.

4. Transfer cauliflower slices to a serving dish. Drizzle with lemon juice and oil. Sprinkle with chipotle, cilantro, and salt. Serve immediately.

Smoked Okra

Smoked okra can be sliced, breaded, and fried to accompany any type of po' boy sandwich. You'll need soaked skewers for this recipe.

INGREDIENTS | SERVES 8

1 pound okra
1 tablespoon vegetable oil
¾ teaspoon kosher or sea salt
¾ teaspoon dry rub

1. Set up grill for direct heat. Preheat grill to medium-high. Presoak bamboo skewers in water for 30 minutes.

2. In a medium bowl or plastic bag, toss okra in vegetable oil. Add salt and dry rub and toss again. Thread okra across two soaked bamboo skewers. Leave a little space between each piece of okra.

3. Add a handful of wood chips or pellets directly to the heat source. Immediately grill okra on hot grill over smoking wood chips until tender and charred, about 4 minutes per side.

Smoked Veggie Loaf

Lentils and brown rice absorb smoke flavor very well. You can turn this recipe from vegetarian to vegan by using an egg substitute for the eggs. Also, instead of a loaf, you can make patties for a nice vegetarian hamburger.

INGREDIENTS | SERVES 6

3 cups cooked lentils, mashed

¼ cup wheat germ

1 cup whole wheat bread crumbs

½ cup cooked brown rice

1 onion, minced

3 cloves garlic, minced

3 eggs

1 teaspoon dried oregano leaves

1 teaspoon dried thyme leaves

1 tablespoon soy sauce

¼ cup ketchup

1 tablespoon olive oil

½ teaspoon hot sauce

½ teaspoon kosher or sea salt

⅛ teaspoon white pepper

1. Set up smoker or grill for indirect heat cooking. Preheat to medium. Use a smoke bomb (see instructions in Chapter 3) or smoker box to generate smoke. Spray a baking sheet with nonstick cooking spray.

2. In a large bowl, combine all ingredients. Transfer mixture to baking sheet and form into a loaf shape.

3. Place on smoker and cook for 45 minutes or until heated through and firm to the touch.

Smoked Vegetable Grilled Focaccia Pizza

The only real work involved in this recipe is in preparing the vegetables. Not only will they work great on a pizza, but there will be enough flavor to make them a good side dish as well.

INGREDIENTS | SERVES 4

1 large white onion, peeled and halved

1½ pound tomatoes, halved

1 head garlic, top removed

3 tablespoons olive oil, divided

2 tablespoons dried herbs: any combination of rosemary, oregano, or thyme

1 teaspoon kosher or sea salt

1 (9" × 12") sheet focaccia bread or prebaked pizza crust

6 ounces soft goat cheese

1. Set up grill for indirect heat cooking and preheat to low. Use a smoke bomb (see instructions in Chapter 3) or smoker box to generate smoke.

2. Place onions, tomatoes, and garlic on a baking sheet. Drizzle with 2 tablespoons of olive oil and season with herbs and salt. Cook in a covered grill or smoker for 1 hour or until the vegetables have caramelized. Allow to cool slightly.

3. Coarsely chop onion and tomatoes. Scoop the softened garlic from the head. Set aside.

4. Lightly coat the bottom of the focaccia or pizza crust with remaining olive oil. Top with goat cheese and grilled vegetables. Return to grill and toast lightly, using the remaining heat from the coals of a charcoal grill or very low heat on a gas grill.

CHAPTER 13

Desserts and Treats

Looking to impress your guests during your next barbecue? Try smoking dessert. There are a number of delicious sweet treats that you can make in your smoker—try experimenting to see what works for you. You can start with fruits that are usually cooked in the oven. Most often these fruits become part of a dessert, like a pie, tart, or cobbler. Adding smoke, whether on the smoker or on the grill, is a great way to take the dessert cooking out of the kitchen and into the backyard. If you can cook it in the oven, you can smoke it outdoors.

▼ GRILLING FRUIT TIMES

Fruit	Heat Source	Time
Apples, ½-inch slices	Medium/Direct	4–6 minutes
Apricots, pitted and halved	Medium/Direct	6–8 minutes
Bananas, halved lengthwise	Medium/Direct	6–8 minutes
Peaches, pitted and halved	Medium/Direct	8–10 minutes
Pears, halved	Medium/Direct	8–10 minutes
Pineapple, ½-inch rings	Medium/Direct	7–10 minutes

RECIPES

Grilled Pound Cake with Berries

The caramelized sugars in this cake along with the flavor of the grilled butter makes this a perfect, light summertime dessert. Grill up some extra slices of pound cake, allow to cool, and then freeze for later.

INGREDIENTS | SERVES 6

1 cup sliced fresh strawberries

1 cup fresh raspberries

1 cup fresh blueberries

5 tablespoons sugar, divided

1 tablespoon minced fresh mint

1 cup heavy whipping cream

1 tablespoon lemon juice

1 teaspoon grated lemon zest

3 tablespoons butter, softened

6 slices pound cake (about 1-inch thick)

1. Combine strawberries, raspberries, blueberries, 2 tablespoons sugar, and mint in a large bowl. Set aside.

2. Using an electric mixer, beat cream in a small bowl until it begins to thicken. While beating, slowly add remaining 3 tablespoons of sugar. Add lemon juice and lemon zest and beat until soft peaks are formed. Cover and refrigerate until ready to serve.

3. Set up grill for direct cooking and preheat to medium. Butter both sides of pound cake slices. Grill, uncovered, for 1–2 minutes on each side or until the slices are a light golden brown. Top pound cake with reserved berries and whipped cream.

Fruit-and-Cake Kebabs

This colorful and flavorful dessert is a hit with all ages. Kids will especially enjoy the experience of eating fruit and cake on a stick. If you don't like apricot, you can substitute a different kind of fruit preserves.

INGREDIENTS | SERVES 6

½ cup apricot preserves

1 tablespoon water

1 tablespoon butter

⅛ teaspoon ground cinnamon

⅛ teaspoon ground nutmeg

3 medium nectarines, pitted and quartered

3 medium plums, pitted and quartered

3 medium peaches, pitted and quartered

1 (10¾-ounce) loaf pound cake, cut into 2-inch cubes

1. Combine apricot preserves, water, butter, cinnamon, and nutmeg in a small saucepan over medium heat. Stir until well blended, about 5 minutes.

2. Set up grill for direct cooking and preheat to medium.

3. Thread fruit and cake onto bamboo skewers, alternating between fruit and cubes of cake.

4. Grill, uncovered, for 1–2 minutes on each side or until cake is a light golden brown and the fruit is tender, but not mushy. Brush with apricot preserve mixture. Remove from grill and serve.

Bread Pudding

To give this bread pudding a smoky taste, open the foil slightly for 10 minutes or so at the beginning of the cooking process or lightly toast the bread on the grill before cutting it into cubes. Serve with a scoop of Simply Marvelous Brown Sugar Ice Cream (see recipe in this chapter).

INGREDIENTS | SERVES 4

2 eggs

1 cup milk

½ cup sugar

¼ teaspoon cinnamon

4 cups bread cubes

1 cup blackberries or you favorite type of berry

1. Set up grill for indirect heat cooking and preheat to medium-high heat.

2. In a medium bowl, whisk eggs until slightly frothy. Whisk in milk, sugar, and cinnamon until blended. Add bread cubes and berries and stir until mixed. Cover and refrigerate for 30 minutes.

3. Butter 6 sheets of foil about 12" × 12". Divide bread mixture into 6 equal servings. Place one serving in the middle of each sheet of foil. Fold over ends of the foil and seal to form a packet. Grill packets over indirect heat for 35 minutes, turning several times.

4. Remove packets from grill and allow to rest 5 minutes before opening.

Mini Grilled Pineapple Upside-Down Cakes

These simple mini upside-down cakes are easy to make and taste fantastic. The shortcake shells are usually found in the produce department near the strawberries.

INGREDIENTS | SERVES 1

1 tablespoon butter
1½ tablespoons brown sugar
1 pineapple ring
1 maraschino cherry
1 small shortcake shell

1. Set up grill for indirect heat cooking and preheat to medium.

2. Spray a sheet of foil, big enough to hold the quantity of upside-down cakes you plan to cook, with nonstick cooking spray. Place butter in the middle of the foil sheet and top with brown sugar.

3. Set pineapple ring on the brown sugar and place a maraschino cherry in the center of the pineapple ring. Top the pineapple with the shortcake shell.

4. Fold sides of the foil up to form a packet. Loosely crimp the foil so it stays sealed, but with enough space to allow steam to escape.

5. Grill with indirect heat for 10–12 minutes, butter-and-sugar side down. Remove from grill, turn over, open foil slightly, and allow to rest 5 minutes. Serve.

Simply Marvelous Brown Sugar Ice Cream

You can find Simply Marvelous rub at www.bigpoppasmokers.com, or if you'd like, just use one of your favorite sweet and spicy barbecue rubs.

INGREDIENTS | SERVES 4

4 egg yolks

1 cup packed light brown sugar

1 cup heavy cream

3 cups half-and-half or light cream

1 tablespoon Simply Marvelous Sweet and Spicy Rub

1½ teaspoons vanilla extract

1. In a medium, heavy, nonaluminum bowl, whisk together the egg yolks and brown sugar until thick.

2. In another medium saucepan, bring the cream, half-and-half, and rub just to a boil over medium heat. Gradually whisk the hot cream into the egg yolk mixture in a thin stream. Cook over low heat, stirring constantly, until the custard is thick enough to coat the back of a spoon (about 6 minutes). Do not allow the mixture to boil.

3. Immediately strain the custard into a medium bowl. Stir in the vanilla and cool to room temperature, stirring occasionally, about 30 minutes. Cover and refrigerate until very cold (at least 5 hours).

4. Pour the cold custard into an ice cream maker and freeze according to the manufacturer's instructions. Let the ice cream soften slightly before serving.

Banana Dessert Quesadilla

Grilled bananas, gooey chocolate, ice cream, and just a hint of heat from the chipotle powder make this one of the most unusual and delicious desserts you can make on the grill.

INGREDIENTS | SERVES 4

3 tablespoons firmly packed brown sugar, plus more for top

¼ teaspoon ground cinnamon

⅛ teaspoon chipotle powder

2 (10-inch) flour tortillas

2 tablespoons butter, melted

1 medium banana, peeled and thinly sliced

¼ cup semisweet chocolate morsels

1 cup vanilla ice cream

¼ cup caramel sauce

1 tablespoon grated dark chocolate

1. Preheat the grill to medium heat. Spray the grill rack with cooking spray. Combine brown sugar, cinnamon, and chipotle powder in a small bowl and set aside.

2. Brush one side of a tortilla with melted butter. Place the tortilla on the grill, buttered side down. Arrange the banana slices on the tortilla and top evenly with the chocolate morsels. Sprinkle with the brown sugar mixture.

3. Place the remaining tortilla on top to cover the bananas. Brush with more butter and sprinkle some brown sugar on top. Grill until the chocolate is melted and the bananas are soft, 3–4 minutes per side. Remove from grill.

4. Cut into wedges and serve with ice cream, caramel sauce, and grated chocolate.

Grilled Peaches with Sweetened Sour Cream

The natural sugars in the peaches will caramelize. When they combine with the sweet and sourness of the sour cream, you'll have a tasty dessert. The crushed amaretti cookies provide the crunch. If you don't like the amaretti cookies, give shortbread or ginger snaps a try.

INGREDIENTS | SERVES 4

½ cup sour cream
1 tablespoon light brown sugar
2 large peaches, halved and pitted
1 cup crushed amaretti cookies

Choosing Peaches for the Grill

The best way to tell if a peach is good for the grill is to smell it and then gently squeeze it. It should have a fragrant aroma, and when lightly pressed with a finger, it should yield slightly. If the peach is hard or mushy, leave it in the store.

1. Set up grill for direct heat and preheat to medium-high.

2. Mix sour cream and brown sugar together in a small bowl. Cover and refrigerate until ready to serve.

3. Grill peaches, cut side down, until warmed through and grill marks start to form (about 8 minutes). Remove peaches from grill.

4. To serve, place ¼ cup crushed cookies in a dessert dish. Top with a grilled peach half. Top with a dollop of sweetened sour cream. Serve immediately.

Pig Candy

This sweet, smoky, and salty treat is great on its own, but it's wonderful when chopped and sprinkled on ice cream, brownies, or any other dessert.

INGREDIENTS | SERVES 4

1 cup dark brown sugar
1 teaspoon chipotle powder
1 pound thick-cut bacon (about 10 slices)

1. Preheat smoker to 235°F.

2. Mix brown sugar and chipotle powder in a small bowl.

3. Lay bacon on a cooking rack. Sprinkle slices with half the brown sugar mixture. Place in smoker and cook for about 45 minutes or until the bacon starts to crisp and the brown sugar melts and forms a crust.

4. Turn bacon over and top with the remainder of the brown sugar mixture. Cook for another 45 minutes or until bacon is crisp. Remove from heat and allow to cool before serving.

Bananas Celeste

Use these sweet grilled bananas in a banana split or sundae, or just eat them right off the grill. Sprinkle them with chocolate powder and a little whipped cream, and you'll be in banana heaven.

INGREDIENTS | SERVES 2

¼ cup turbinado sugar

1 teaspoon ground cinnamon

2 firm, ripe bananas

1. Prepare grill for direct heat cooking and preheat to medium-hot.

2. In a small bowl, combine the sugar and cinnamon. Set aside.

3. Cut the ends off of each banana and split down the middle. Leave the skins on. This will make flipping the bananas on the grill a little easier.

4. Put the bananas, skin side down, on a very hot, oiled grill. Sprinkle cinnamon-sugar mixture over the flesh of the banana. Cover and cook until the banana skin starts to blacken. Flip over to caramelize the sugar. Flip back over and remove from grill.

Smoked Apple Pie

Smoked apple pie—it's better than you think. Give it a try and you'll be surprised. Once you do, you'll never look at your smoker the same way.

INGREDIENTS | SERVES 8

8 cups apple slices (about 7 medium apples)

1 tablespoon fresh lemon juice

½ cup sugar

2 tablespoons flour

1 teaspoon ground cinnamon

¼ teaspoon ground nutmeg

Pastry crust for double crust pie

¼ cup melted apple jelly

1–2 tablespoons heavy (whipping) cream

1. Preheat grill for indirect, high heat or heat a smoker to 400°F.

2. Combine apple slices, lemon juice, sugar, flour, cinnamon, and nutmeg in a large bowl.

3. Roll dough into two 11-inch circles. Place one pastry circle in a 9-inch pie plate. Brush pie dough with the melted apple jelly. Add the apples to the pie shell. Top with second pie circle. Seal edges. Make a few slits in the top crust. Lightly brush the top of the pie with the cream.

4. Bake in the smoker or on the grill for about 40 minutes or until the top is brown and apples are cooked through. Serve warm or at room temperature.

Smoked Almonds

Smoked almonds can be eaten as a tasty snack, but they are also great if you slice or chop them and use them as ingredients in other dishes. Use sliced smoked almonds as a topping for salads or grilled vegetables to add a little smokiness.

INGREDIENTS | SERVES 2

1½ cups raw, skin-on almonds

2 cups hickory wood chips or wood pellets, divided

2 teaspoons olive or canola oil

¼ teaspoon kosher or sea salt, plus more as needed

⅛ teaspoon sugar, plus more as needed

1. Using a sharp knife or Phillips screwdriver, punch holes in the bottom of a 9" × 9" square aluminum pan. Place almonds in the pan in a single layer.

2. Split 2 cups of wood chips into equal parts. Make 2 smoke bombs (see instructions in Chapter 3). Set aside.

3. Prepare the grill for indirect cooking by dumping one chimney of charcoal (about 2 pounds) into your grill. Using tongs, stack briquettes up against one side of the grill. Next, light two charcoal briquettes.

4. Once the two briquettes are lit and completely ashed over, use tongs to carefully place one briquette at each end of the stack of unlit briquettes. Place the two foil packets of chips next to, but not quite touching, the lit briquettes. Open the bottom vents of your grill half way. Place the pan with almonds as far away from the charcoal briquettes that are in the grill. Close the lid and open the top vent about a quarter of the way.

5. The lit briquette will slowly start to burn the unlit briquettes, which in turn will cause the packets of chips to slowly smolder, imparting just a little smoke at a time. Adjust the top vent to control the airflow and temperature and keep the temperature under 100°F. This will give you plenty of time to control the amount of smoke flavor you give the almonds. Usually 2 hours is more than enough smoke.

6. Remove the almonds and serve immediately or store in an airtight container for up to 30 days.

Smoked Snack Mix

Take the traditional crunchy cereal mix and add a barbecue twist with dry rub and smoke.

INGREDIENTS | SERVES 20

6 tablespoons melted unsalted butter

2 tablespoons Worcestershire sauce

1 tablespoon barbecue dry rub (see recipes in Chapter 5)

4½ cups Rice Chex cereal

1 cup small pretzels

1 cup broken bagel chips

1 cup mixed roasted nuts

1. In a small bowl, combine butter, Worcestershire sauce, and dry rub.

2. In a large bowl, combine cereal, pretzels, bagel chips, and nuts. Mix with your hands or two large wooden spoons. Pour butter mixture over the top and gently stir to coat all the dry ingredients with the butter mixture.

3. Place mixture on a baking sheet and spread out evenly. Smoke in your smoker with a mild wood like apple, peach, or cherry for 1 hour. Stir or shake the mixture every 15 minutes.

4. Increase the temperature of the smoker to 350°F. Smoke the mixture until dry, about 20 minutes. (You can also place baking sheet in the oven and bake at 350°F for the same amount of time.)

5. Store in an airtight container in the refrigerator for up to a week.

Smoked Dried Fruit

Try chopping these pieces of dried and smoked fruit to use as a topping for salads. You can also add them to dressings or stuffing when cooking poultry. And, believe it or not, they make a great addition to cereal and oatmeal.

INGREDIENTS | SERVES 4

2 cups dried apricots, peaches, bananas, or apples (or a mixture of two or more)

1. Prepare a stovetop smoker with wood chips according to the manufacturer's instructions.

2. Smoke the dried fruit in the stovetop smoker for 15–20 minutes.

3. Remove from smoker and store in a resealable plastic bag for up to 7 days.

CHAPTER 14

Plank Grilling

Plank grilling is a great way to influence the flavor of your food with different kinds of smoke. While some of the most popular woods to use for plank grilling are mesquite, apple, and maple wood, you can try out a variety of woods and see if you like the flavor they impart to your food. After all, the only way you'll know if you like the smoke a certain wood produces is to try it. As mentioned in Chapter 4, it is very important to stay away from coniferous tree wood such as pine when choosing your planking wood. In addition, don't use abandoned or chemically treated wood for smoking. Always head to the hardware or barbecue store to purchase your wood.

RECIPES

Plank-Smoked Bacon-Wrapped Mushrooms

This simple, yet tasty appetizer will disappear off the plate in no time at all. Make more than you think, because you're going to need it.

INGREDIENTS | SERVES 8

2 large, untreated wood grilling planks

1 pound button mushrooms, cleaned and stemmed

1 pound thin-sliced apple-smoked bacon, each slice cut in half

1. Soak planks and set up your grill for plank smoking as described in Chapter 3. Preheat the planks.

2. Wrap each button mushroom in half a slice of bacon, and secure with a toothpick.

3. Place bacon-wrapped mushrooms on preheated planks. Close grill lid and smoke mushrooms for about 20 minutes.

4. Remove to a platter and serve immediately.

Plank-Smoked Pork Tenderloin

The lightness of the apple or peach wood smoke is a great complement to the earthiness of the pork. Don't be afraid to serve the pork slightly pink. The new USDA standard for pork is to cook it to an internal temperature of 145°F with a 4-minute rest time.

INGREDIENTS | SERVES 8

1 large, untreated wood grilling plank
¼ cup teriyaki sauce
½ cup barbecue sauce
1 (2-pound) boneless pork loin
1 teaspoon kosher or sea salt
1 teaspoon freshly ground black pepper
1 tablespoon olive oil

1. Soak plank and set up your grill for plank smoking as described in Chapter 3. Preheat the plank.

2. In a small bowl, combine teriyaki sauce and barbecue sauce. Set aside. Season the pork loin with salt and pepper.

3. Brush olive oil over the preheated plank to coat. Place pork loin on preheated plank. Close grill and smoke pork for 40 minutes. Brush with a thin layer of the teriyaki and barbecue sauce mixture. Repeat 2 or 3 times every 5 minutes. Continue cooking pork for another 20 minutes, or until the internal temperature reaches 145°F.

4. Remove plank and pork loin from grill and allow to rest 5 minutes. Place wood plank with loin on a platter, slice, and serve.

Plank-Smoked Salmon

The easiest way to tell if salmon is fully cooked is to look closely at the surface of the fillet. When the surface fat turns white, it's done.

INGREDIENTS | SERVES 4

1 large, untreated wood grilling plank

½ cup brown sugar

2 tablespoons olive oil

1 tablespoon dried thyme

1 teaspoon cayenne pepper

1 (2-pound) skin-on salmon fillet

1. Soak plank and set up your grill for plank smoking as described in Chapter 3. Preheat the plank.

2. In a small bowl, combine brown sugar, oil, thyme, and cayenne. Place salmon fillet on a baking sheet and pour mixture over the salmon. Spread over the top of the salmon so it covers the whole fillet.

3. Place salmon on the preheated plank and cook on a covered grill until the salmon is done (about 40 minutes). Remove from the grill, allow to rest 5 minutes, and serve.

Plank-Smoked Flank Steak

This steak is perfect not only served sliced, but will also make a fantastic sandwich or a topping for a bowl of mixed greens.

INGREDIENTS | SERVES 6

1 large, untreated wood grilling plank
½ cup balsamic vinaigrette
½ cup finely chopped onion
½ cup chopped fresh parsley
¼ cup chopped cilantro
2 garlic cloves, minced
1 dash crushed red pepper flakes
1 beef flank steak, about 1½ pounds
1 tablespoon canola oil

1. Soak plank and set up your grill for plank smoking as described in Chapter 3. Preheat the plank.

2. Place vinaigrette, onion, parsley, cilantro, garlic, and red pepper flakes in a small bowl. Whisk to combine. Set aside ½ cup of the mixture. Pour the rest of the dressing mixture into a large resealable plastic bag. Add steak to the bag and seal, squeezing out as much air as possible. Turn bag over a couple of times to coat steak. Refrigerate at least 2 hours to marinate.

3. Remove steak from bag and discard remaining marinade. Brush the top of the preheated plank with oil to coat. Place steak on top of oiled wood plank. Smoke steak for 15–20 minutes or until the internal temperature of the steak reaches 135°F (for medium-rare).

4. Remove steak from plank and turn grill up to high. Sear both sides of steak on the hot grill for 3 minutes per side or until grill marks appear. Remove from grill, cover with foil, and allow to rest for 5 minutes. Slice steak into thin diagonal slices and pour reserved vinaigrette mixture over slices. Serve immediately.

Plank-Smoked Corn on the Cob

Sweet corn takes on the flavor of smoke very easily. Use a spicy dry rub to complement the sweetness.

INGREDIENTS | SERVES 8

2 or 3 large fruit wood grilling planks

8 whole ears of white sweet corn, husks and silk removed

¼ cup olive oil

3 tablespoons dry rub

1. Soak planks and set up your grill for plank smoking as described in Chapter 3. Preheat the planks.

2. Soak corn in cold water for 30 minutes. Remove from water and dry with a towel.

3. Rub each ear of corn with olive oil and season with dry rub. Set aside for 5 minutes.

4. Place ears of corn on the preheated planks, close grill lid, and cook until tender (about 20 minutes). Remove from grill and serve immediately.

Plank-Smoked Mashed Potatoes

What's not to like about potatoes, cheese, cream, and butter? These delicious potatoes will get you loads of compliments from your friends and guests.

INGREDIENTS | SERVES 8

8 large Yukon gold potatoes, peeled and quartered

2 tablespoons unsalted butter

½ cup heavy cream

⅓ cup chopped fresh chives

2 or 3 large, untreated wood grilling planks

6 sticks of string cheese, cut into ¾-inch cubes

1. Bring a large pot of heavily salted water to a boil over high heat. Add potatoes and cook until tender (about 15 minutes). Drain well in a colander. Allow to set in colander for 15 minutes for any excess water to evaporate.

2. In a small saucepan over medium heat, melt butter. Add cream and stir to mix well. Reduce heat to low and keep warm.

3. Place the potatoes back in the pot and add the butter mixture and chives. Mash potatoes, leaving a few lumps. Cool mashed potatoes to room temperature, cover, and refrigerate until ready to cook.

4. Soak planks and set up your grill for plank smoking as described in Chapter 3. Preheat the planks.

5. Remove potatoes from the refrigerator and allow to warm slightly at room temperature. Mix string cheese cubes into the mashed potatoes. Form uniform-size mounds of mashed potatoes and place on preheated wood planks.

6. Smoke on grill for 15–20 minutes, until potatoes are warmed all the way through and tops of each mound begin to brown. Remove from planks to a platter or serving plates. Serve immediately.

Plank-Smoked Cheddar Biscuits

These biscuits are a fantastic addition to just about any meal.

INGREDIENTS | SERVES 6

1 large, untreated wood grilling plank
¾ cup buttermilk
1 cup shredded sharp Cheddar cheese
1 tablespoon fresh sage, chopped
½ teaspoon freshly ground black pepper
1¾ cups all-purpose flour
1 tablespoon baking powder
1 tablespoon sugar
¼ teaspoon kosher or sea salt
½ cup unsalted butter, cold

1. Soak plank and set up your grill for plank smoking as described in Chapter 3. Preheat the grill.

2. In a small bowl combine the buttermilk, cheese, sage, and black pepper. Set aside.

3. In a large bowl combine flour, baking powder, sugar, and salt. Using a pastry cutter or two knives, cut in the cold butter until the mixture forms coarse crumbs. Make a well in the middle of the mixture in the bowl. Add the buttermilk mixture to the well and stir until moistened.

4. Turn dough out onto a lightly floured bread board or counter. Knead dough, folding in half between strokes. Knead until the dough stays together (about 6 strokes).

5. Press dough down gently until it forms a 6-inch square about 1-inch thick. Cut dough into 3-inch rounds using a pastry ring.

6. Place biscuits on prepared wood plank. Grill, covered, for 15–20 minutes or until biscuits are golden brown.

Glossary of Smoking and Cooking Terms

Barbecue

Cooking outdoors using smoke for additional flavor over low temperatures for a long period of time. Variations include BBQ, Bar-B-Cue, Bar-B-Que, Barbeque, Que, or Q.

Bark

A crunchy crust that forms on some foods while cooking. The color can be anywhere from brown to almost black. Bark is the result of a variety of reactions to the seasonings used, dehydration of the meat, and the Maillard reaction.

Brine

The process of submerging meat, vegetables, and seafood in a heavily salted solution prior to cooking. Brining adds moisture to the food and can also be used to add additional flavors.

Butterflying

See *Spatchcock*.

Ceramic Cooker

A cooker made from clay or other ceramic materials. Typically manufactured in a shape similar to an egg, the ceramic cooker has been used by a variety of cultures for hundreds of years.

Charcoal, Briquette

A type of charcoal formed by compressing a mixture of charred wood products. May contain other materials like binders and accelerants.

Charcoal, Lump

A carbonized or charred wood product that is created by exposing wood to high heat without very much oxygen. Charcoal will usually burn at a stable temperature.

Charcuterie

The art of curing, preserving, and preparing meats such as bacon, ham, sausage, and other meats.

Cold Smoking

Smoking foods, such as cheese, fish, and some charcuterie, at temperatures below 140°F.

Collagen

The connective tissues in meats that melt after long cooking to tenderize the meat.

Dice

To cut food into small pieces, generally between ⅛- and ¼-inch in size.

Fat Cap

The thick layer of fat found on the top of some cuts of meat.

Firebox

The part of the smoker or pit that contains the heat and generates the smoke. Fireboxes are used in indirect heat cooking.

Fork Tender

A term to describe the texture of cooked food. A fork pushed into the food will slide out smoothly without resistance.

Grate

The part of a grill over the heat source on which the food is placed for cooking.

Grill

A type of cooker primarily designed for high, direct heat cooking using either charcoal or gas. Grills can also be adapted for indirect heat cooking and smoking.

Hardwood

The species of woods that do not contain resins. These woods are typically harder than wood species that contain resins. Hardwoods provide better-tasting smoke and burn longer and cleaner.

Hot-and-Fast

Cooking with higher temperatures, typically over 325°F.

Liquid Propane (LP)

A type of compressed gas in liquid form used for backyard grills.

Low-and-Slow

Cooking at lower temperatures, typically between 225°F and 275°F.

Marbling

The fat within the meat. Usually, the more marbling, the more tender, juicy, and flavorful the meat is.

Marinade

A liquid meant to tenderize or add flavor to meats. Marinades are typically lower in salt than brines but include more acid and oil.

Membrane

The skin found on the underside, or bone side, of a rack of ribs.

Mop Sauce

A thin, watery mixture, usually vinegar based, that is mopped on the meat surface while it is being smoked.

Render/Rendering

The process of melting fats.

Rest

Allowing the meat to sit after cooking, usually tented in foil, to allow the meat to reabsorb some of its juices. This results in a more moist meat.

Rub, Dry

A mixture of spices or other seasonings that are rubbed into the meat before cooking.

Rub, Wet
Spices or other seasonings mixed with a liquid and then rubbed into the meat before cooking.

Salt, Curing
A salt used in curing meats that contains added sodium nitrate and sometimes sodium nitrite. Also known as Prague powder.

Salt, Kosher
A salt used in cooking that contains no additives. The term *kosher* comes from the salt used to make meats kosher.

Salt, Pickling
A very fine-grain salt that dissolves quickly, with no additives or anti-caking products.

Salt, Sea
A cooking salt made from evaporating sea water. Sea salt naturally has no additives.

Salt, Table
Also called common salt, it often has additives such as iodine.

Seasoned Wood
Smoked woods that have been aged or dried.

Smoke Bomb
A packet of wood chips created with foil to generate wood smoke, usually on a grill.

Smoker Box
A metal or cast-iron box used for holding wood chips when smoking foods.

Smoke Ring
A layer of light red or pink color that forms below the bark of smoked meats.

Smoker

A generic term used to describe a device used to smoke food.

Spatchcock

Cutting the backbone out of a chicken or turkey so that it lays flat on the grill, which allows for quicker cooking.

Stall

A period of time when the internal temperature of meat does not rise during cooking. This is a temporary stage.

Zone Cooking

The technique of setting up a grill or smoker with multiple temperature zones, giving the cook more flexibility and control of the cooking process. This is typically done as two zones: one hot (direct heat) and one cooler (indirect heat).

APPENDIX B

Additional Resources

Smoke Woods

Baxter's Original Premium Smoking Woods
A large selection of small batch–prepared smoke woods
www.baxtersoriginal.com

Fruita Wood
Premium select hardwoods
www.fruitawoodchunks.com

The Grilling Plank Superstore
Wood grilling planks in all sizes and shapes
www.grillingplanks.biz

Maine Grilling Woods
Great traditional and oval wood planks
www.mainegrillingwoods.com

Online Barbecue Supply Stores

BBQ Addicts
Great seasoning and sauces and home of the Bacon Explosion
www.bbqaddicts.com

Big Poppa Smokers
Anything and everything to do with smoking outdoors
www.bigpoppasmokers.com

The Kansas City BBQ Store
The world's largest selection of barbecue supplies
www.thekansascitybbqstore.com

Tasty Licks BBQ Supply
Music and barbecue . . . a good combination
www.fredsmusicandbbq.com

US BBQ Supply
A nice new online retailer
www.usbbqsupply.com

Seasonings and Rubs

Albukirky Seasonings
Great seasonings with a taste of the Southwest
www.albukirkyseasonings.com

Dizzy Pig
A flavor for just about everyone
www.dizzypigbbq.com

Tatonka Dust
An original steak seasoning
www.owensbbq.com

Todd's Dirt
Makes getting dirty tasty
www.toddsdirt.com

Smoked Food–Related Blogs

Amazing Ribs
A crazy amount of information
www.amazingribs.com

Embers & Flame
All about outdoor cooking
www.embersandflame.com

Full Custom Gospel BBQ
All about Texas barbecue
www.fcg-bbq.blogspot.com

Nibble Me This

One of the best all-around outdoor cooking blogs

www.nibblemethis.com

No Excuses BBQ

Quirky, yet educational

www.noexcusesbbq.com

Scott Roberts

All about spicy foods

www.scottrobertsweb.com

Smoked Food Forums

BBQ Brethren

Without a doubt the best barbecue forum in the world

www.bbq-brethren.com

The BBQ Forum

Been around since 1995

www.rbjb.com/rbjb/rbjbboard/

Big Green Eggs Forum

All about ceramic smokers

www.greeneggers.com

Texas BBQ Forum

Discussions centered around Texas barbecue

www.texasbbqforum.com

The Virtual Weber Bullet

All about the Weber Smokey Mountain Cooker

www.virtualweberbullet.com

Miscellaneous Sites

A-MAZE-N Tube Smoker
Great tool for generating cold smoke
www.amazenproducts.com

Amazon
If they don't have it, you don't need it
www.amazon.com

Huwa Reserve Beef
Fantastic natural-raised beef from Colorado
www.huwareserve.com

Mac's BBQ
Innovative smoker products
www.macsbbq.com

Smoke Daddy
Cold smoke generator
www.smokedaddyinc.com

Williams-Sonoma
A great source for gourmet products for indoor smoking
www.williams-sonoma.com

The Wok Shop
Woks make great outdoor smokers
www.wokshop.com

Cowgirl's Country Life
How to build a smokehouse
http://cowgirlscountry.blogspot.com/2008/01/building-cold-smoker-smoke-house.html

Standard U.S./Metric Measurement Conversions

VOLUME CONVERSIONS

U.S. Volume Measure	Metric Equivalent
⅛ teaspoon	0.5 milliliter
¼ teaspoon	1 milliliter
½ teaspoon	2 milliliters
1 teaspoon	5 milliliters
½ tablespoon	7 milliliters
1 tablespoon (3 teaspoons)	15 milliliters
2 tablespoons (1 fluid ounce)	30 milliliters
¼ cup (4 tablespoons)	60 milliliters
⅓ cup	90 milliliters
½ cup (4 fluid ounces)	125 milliliters
⅔ cup	160 milliliters
¾ cup (6 fluid ounces)	180 milliliters
1 cup (16 tablespoons)	250 milliliters
1 pint (2 cups)	500 milliliters
1 quart (4 cups)	1 liter (about)

WEIGHT CONVERSIONS

U.S. Weight Measure	Metric Equivalent
½ ounce	15 grams
1 ounce	30 grams
2 ounces	60 grams
3 ounces	85 grams
¼ pound (4 ounces)	115 grams
½ pound (8 ounces)	225 grams
¾ pound (12 ounces)	340 grams
1 pound (16 ounces)	454 grams

OVEN TEMPERATURE CONVERSIONS

Degrees Fahrenheit	Degrees Celsius
200 degrees F	95 degrees C
250 degrees F	120 degrees C
275 degrees F	135 degrees C
300 degrees F	150 degrees C
325 degrees F	160 degrees C
350 degrees F	180 degrees C
375 degrees F	190 degrees C
400 degrees F	205 degrees C
425 degrees F	220 degrees C
450 degrees F	230 degrees C

BAKING PAN SIZES

U.S.	Metric
8 × 1½ inch round baking pan	20 × 4 cm cake tin
9 × 1½ inch round baking pan	23 × 3.5 cm cake tin
11 × 7 × 1½ inch baking pan	28 × 18 × 4 cm baking tin
13 × 9 × 2 inch baking pan	30 × 20 × 5 cm baking tin
2 quart rectangular baking dish	30 × 20 × 3 cm baking tin
15 × 10 × 2 inch baking pan	30 × 25 × 2 cm baking tin (Swiss roll tin)
9 inch pie plate	22 × 4 or 23 × 4 cm pie plate
7 or 8 inch springform pan	18 or 20 cm springform or loose-bottom cake tin
9 × 5 × 3 inch loaf pan	23 × 13 × 7 cm or 2 lb narrow loaf or pâté tin
1½ quart casserole	1.5 liter casserole
2 quart casserole	2 liter casserole

Index